The Real Jesus

The Real Jesus

Then and Now

Geza Vermes

Fortress Press

Minneapolis

Library of Congress Cataloging-in-Publication Data
Vermes, Geza, 1924-
  The real Jesus : then and now / Geza Vermes.
      p. cm.
  Includes bibliographical references.
  ISBN 978-0-8006-9763-1 (alk. paper)
  1. Jesus Christ. 2. Christianity. I. Title.
  BT199.V47 2010
  232—dc22
                                                    2010012484

The paper used in this publication meets the minimum require-
ments of American National Standard for Information Sciences
— Permanence of Paper for Printed Library Materials, ANSI
Z329.48-1984.

Manufactured in the U.S.A.
14   13   12   11   10   1   2   3   4   5   6   7   8   9   10

Contents

Preface

In years gone by, not a few university colleagues of mine have considered it below their dignity to engage in what the French call *haute vulgarisation*, the presentation of complicated issues of scholarship to a broad readership avoiding the use of technical jargon and requiring no prior familiarity with the subject. This attitude, in which obscurity parades as profundity and lack of perspicacity is assumed to indicate advanced learning, often derives from the inability of specialists to express themselves with clarity and simplicity. I would like to think that I was born with the gift of easy communication, being the son of a life-long journalist. The smell of the printer's ink is among my early childhood memories and, at the age of 12, during the Berlin Olympics, I ran the sports column of my father's paper. In 1971, when I began to edit the *Journal of Jewish Studies*, I felt I was reviving the family tradition tragically interrupted in 1944 by the murderous lunacy released on the innocent in Hitler's empire. This background will explain why even my most creative works, like *Jesus the Jew*, were meant to be easily accessible to any educated person interested in the subject. Indeed, on retiring from my Oxford professorship, I expressly vowed to dedicate myself to sharing with the widest possible circles the insights gained through half a century of wrestling with ideas springing from the interaction between Judaism and Christianity.

After my early apprenticeship in the 1930s, I decided in the 1980s and 1990s to try again my hand at writing for the press, but most of my journalistic activity, my addresses at literary festivals as well as my participation in radio programmes and television documentaries date to the twenty-first century. The various bits that follow were originally published in dailies, weeklies and monthlies, especially in *The Times*, the *Independent*, the *Guardian*, the *Daily* and the *Sunday Telegraph*, and *Standpoint*. I must admit that I found journalism's constraint to express myself quickly and in an easily readable style highly exciting and enjoyable.

Friends and above all my wife have prevailed on me to include a selection of them between the covers of a single volume together with lectures and talks which have never appeared previously in print. I am deeply indebted to SCM Press and, in the United States, Fortress Press, publishers of my first Jesus trilogy – *Jesus the Jew, Jesus and the World of Judaism* (renamed *Jesus in his Jewish Context*) and *The Religion of Jesus the Jew* – for undertaking the publication of the present miscellany of essays. I sincerely hope that their admirable courage in these days of financial squeeze will prove worthwhile.

The articles and lectures assembled in this volume, like my preceding scholarly publications, reflect the views on religious matters of a liberal thinker, free of the constraints of churches, synagogues and their secular equivalents, who has tried throughout his life to separate reality from myth. The topics treated in these pages converge on the main themes of my previous academic research: the historical Jesus, his real life and authentic teaching, and the sketching of the genuine portrait of this holy Galilean Jew liberated from the religious images superimposed on it by theological speculations of his non-Jewish followers over two millennia.

Readers familiar with my writings will not be surprised to discover that the study of the Dead Sea Scrolls, 'my first academic love affair', is still firmly represented in this volume, anticipating *The Story of the Scrolls*, a truthful account of Qumran to appear early in 2010. In the present volume will also figure a variety of reflections on Jewish/Christian subjects, ranging from tax-collectors in the age of Jesus to the conclave electing the successor of Pope John Paul II and from the great Da Vinci distraction, to use the headline of *The Times*, to an analysis of the implications of the visit by the son of a Tehran Jewish school caretaker (the president of the State of Israel) to the son of a Bavarian policeman

(Pope Benedict XVI) amid all the pomp and ceremony associated with a Vatican state event.

The reaction of the British press to a TV documentary on Jesus produced by the infant Channel 4 in 1984 may both amaze and amuse readers today. Also they may find appropriate in 2010, the year following the bicentenary of Darwin's birth and the sesqui-centenary of *On the Origin of Species*, some thoughts on the evolution of religious ideas accompanied by lighthearted comments on the constant preoccupation with sex on the part of the elderly celibate clerical leaders of the Roman Catholic Church.

Geza Vermes
Oxford

Part One

Jesus

1

The Age of Jesus

In 1906 Albert Schweitzer solemnly declared the quest for the historical Jesus to be an unattainable task, yet despite his eloquent funeral oration the Jesus of history has refused to lie down or disappear. In fact, with the exception of a handful of inveterate doubters, most present day scholars go to the other extreme and take the existence of Jesus so much for granted that they do not bother to inquire into the meaning of historicity. Yet the truth is that Jesus and the movement which arose in his wake did not exist *in vacuo*: they were integral parts of first-century Jewish society, a society formed by the forces and influences of previous generations and by the impact of Hellenism and of the political power of Rome. These Jewish and Graeco-Roman influences interacted and created the matrix out of which Christianity emerged.

The purpose of this book is to make the reader aware of the amalgam of ideas, inspirations and impulses that penetrated the age of Jesus.[1] To achieve this purpose in a vivid fashion, I have chosen to present a series of biographical vignettes. The wider world will be made tangible through the depiction of individuals, who in their various ways were influential in the making of history. *Who's Who in the Age of Jesus* portrays personalities from the New Testament, from the works of first-century Jewish writers, from rabbinic literature and from the sources of Graeco-Roman history. These personalities occasionally appear in various records. Rulers of Judaea, Jewish leaders and Roman dignitaries such as Herod the Great, Antipas, Annas and Caiaphas, Gamaliel the Elder, Augustus, Tiberius, Pontius Pilate, etc., are mentioned in the New Testament, and some New Testament characters (Jesus, John the Baptist, James the brother of the Lord) make a fleeting appearance in Josephus and in the accounts of Roman historians like Tacitus. Other Jewish characters like Hillel the Elder, Honi and Hanina ben Dosa, Jesus son of Ananias, who are recorded in Josephus or in rabbinic literature, shed important light on the Gospel story. In consequence, a multi-pronged approach to the age of Jesus promises to open up unexpected fresh vistas.

The broader scope thus conceived demands also an elastic definition of the time scale of the inquiry. The net will be cast wider than the presumed life span of Jesus (c. 6/5 BCE–30 CE). One reasonable starting point would be the Maccabaean revolution against the Seleucid (Syrian) Greek Empire in the 160s BCE, when Jews first experienced religious persecution. The forceful and ultimately successful Jewish resistance to Hellenistic tyranny led to the creation of an independent Jewish state, which was governed for the best part of a century (152–63 BCE) by the priestly family of the Maccabees-Hasmonaeans. However, to call 150 years of the pre-Christian era the age of Jesus seems something of an exaggeration. Hence it is preferable to choose instead the next significant watershed in Jewish-international history, the switch from the Seleucid-Greek to the Roman rule in Palestine, inaugurated in 63 BCE by Pompey's conquest of Jerusalem. This happened less than two generations before the birth of Jesus. The ideal finishing line would lie roughly two generations after the crucifixion. However, the absence of any remarkable event in the closing years of the first century CE prompts one to opt for the end of the second Jewish uprising against Rome in 135 CE. These two boundary posts encompass one of the very crucial periods of the intellectual and religious history of the western world.

The 200 years in question can neatly be divided into five stages.

1 From Pompey to the end of the Hasmonaean priestly rule (63–37 BCE).
2 The reign of Herod the Great (37–4 BCE) and the birth of Jesus; Herod Archelaus (4 BCE–6 CE); Roman prefects (6–41 CE), Herod Antipas (4 BCE–39 CE) – the public ministry and death of Jesus (29–30 CE).

3 Agrippa I (41–44 CE); Roman procurators (44–66 CE); First rebellion (66–70 [73/4] CE) – the beginnings of Judaeo-Christianity and career of St Paul.
4 From the fall of Jerusalem to the end of the second rebellion under Hadrian (70–135 CE) – the departure of Christianity from its Jewish social setting.

The Rise and Glory of the Hasmonaeans (164 – 67 BCE)

After two and a half centuries of Babylonian and Persian domination, followed by Greek overlordship introduced by Alexander the Great's conquest of the Near and Middle East, in 164 BCE the Jews recovered their independence and complete self-government owing to their successful armed resistance to the cultural and religious Hellenization imposed on them by the Greek monarch Antiochus IV Epiphanes (175–164 BCE). The Hasmonaean Jewish priestly family of Mattathias and his sons, surnamed the Maccabees, triumphed over the Seleucids of Syria and restored the Jewish worship, which had temporarily been transformed by Antiochus into the cult of Olympian Zeus, whose statue he had installed in the holy place in Jerusalem. The upheaval caused by the Hellenists aided and abetted by Jewish upper class allies inaugurated a feverish anticipation of the final age, of the eschatological and apocalyptic era, which was expected to culminate in the arrival of the final Redeemer, the king Messiah, foretold by the biblical prophets and anxiously awaited by the pious Jews who were dreaming of freedom under God. The victorious Judas Maccabaeus (164–161 BCE) and his brother Jonathan (161–143/2 BCE) defeated the enemy and restored a Jewish state. Jonathan, though not a scion of the sacerdotal dynasty which held the pontificate since the time of King David, proclaimed himself high priest in 153/2 BCE, and Simon, another of the Maccabee brothers, established himself as hereditary religious and political head of the Jewish nation in 143/2 BCE.

His son John Hyrcanus I (135/4–104 BCE) and John's successors, Judas Aristobulus I (104–3 BCE) and Jonathan or Alexander Jannaeus (103–76 BCE) extended the frontiers of the new Jewish

5

state and compelled the neighbouring peoples, the Idumaeans in the south and the various foreign clans in and around Galilee, to recognize them as their rulers and embrace Judaism as their religion. This entailed submission to circumcision as far as the male population was concerned. Their Judaizing missionary activity did not stop these Hasmonaean priest kings from practising harsh secular tyranny at home. Alexander Jannaeus is in particular notorious for his cruelty in wreaking vengeance on his political opponents, the Pharisees. He ordered 800 of them to be crucified while he and his mistresses, eating, drinking and merrymaking, were mesmerized by the unholy spectacle.

On Alexander's death his widow, the pious Shelamzion or Alexandra Salome, a great friend of the Pharisees, occupied the royal throne with her elder son, John Hyrcanus II inheriting the high priesthood (76–67 BCE). His more vigorous and envious younger brother Judas Aristobulus II was however determined to dispossess him of his office. When Queen Alexandra died, civil war broke out between the two priestly rivals and with the ensuing conflict opens a new era leading to the age of Jesus.

From Pompey to the End of the Hasmonaean Priestly Rule (63–37 BCE)

The attempt by Aristobulus II to unseat Hyrcanus II, the legitimate holder of the high priesthood, and the forceful riposte by Hyrcanus, backed by the clever Idumaean strong man Antipater, the father of Herod the Great, and the Nabataean king Aretas III, formed the preamble to the Roman invasion of Judaea by Pompey in 63 BCE. The trio of Hyrcanus, Antipater and Aretas laid siege to Jerusalem where Aristobulus was forced to withdraw. The innocent victim of the battle was the renowned miracle working man of God, Honi, whom the partisans of Hyrcanus stoned to death for refusing to put a curse on Aristobulus and his party. Here we are faced with a politically motivated murder with religious undercurrents. The trend repeated itself in the case of John the Baptist, Jesus, James, the brother of the Lord and others.

The stalemate between the two forces induced both Aristobulus and Hyrcanus to ask for Pompey's intervention. Each hoped to find favour with him. Instead, Pompey, accompanied by the army of his general Marcus Aemilius Scaurus, conquered Jerusalem and without further ado they turned the Hasmonaean state into the Roman province of Judaea. Hyrcanus was reinstalled in the high priesthood, but the title of king was removed from him, while the deposed Aristobulus was sent to Rome as a prisoner. A little later he escaped and began to organize resistance to Rome at home, but he was soon arrested and returned to captivity in the imperial capital. At the start of the Roman civil war between Julius Caesar and Pompey, Caesar released him as he saw in Aristobulus a potential ally, but the Jewish leader was poisoned by Pompey's partisans before he could set sail and support Caesar in Syria.

After the battle of Pharsalus in 48 BCE, where Pompey was defeated, Hyrcanus and Antipater switched their allegiance to the victor. Caesar, who generally showed himself sympathetic to the Jews both in Palestine and in the diaspora, rewarded them by reappointing Hyrcanus II as nominal head of state or ethnarch of the Jews and placing the administration of the province in the hands of the Idumaean Antipater, who shared his duties with his two sons, Phasael and Herod.

While governor of Galilee, the young Herod overstepped the boundaries of legality and ordered without trial the execution of the rebel leader Ezechias and his men. He was summoned before the Jewish Sanhedrin, but with Roman help and the connivance of Hyrcanus, the president of the court, Herod escaped conviction and was confirmed in his position by Caesar's colleague Mark Antony, the Roman plenipotentiary in the eastern Mediterranean provinces. In 40 BCE the mighty Iranian tribe of the Parthians invaded Judaea and gave their patronage to Antigonus, the son of Aristobulus II, and a rival of Hyrcanus II. On his coins, Antigonus called himself high priest and king. To ensure his position as high priest, he maimed his uncle Hyrcanus, apparently by biting off one of his ears, with a view to making him unfit to act as a pontiff. However, the ephemeral rule of Antigonus came to an end in 37 BCE, when the Romans captured and beheaded him by order of Antony, who in 40 BCE had already nominated Herod as king of Judaea. In 37 BCE, after his conquest of Jerusalem with the helping hand of Sosius, the Roman governor of Syria and of his legions, Herod, the Idumaean upstart, actually became the ruler of the Jewish nation and terminated the century-long dominion of the Maccabaean-Hasmonaean dynasty.

The Reign of Herod the Great (37–4 BCE) – The Birth of Jesus (c. 6/5 BCE)

The reign of Herod covers the decades of Jewish history which directly open the 'age of Jesus', who was born shortly before Herod died. The friendly Roman oversight of the government of Judaea and the iron fist of the new monarch substantially affected the Jewish society in which Jesus lived. Herod was a cross between a genius and a monster; he was a master tight-rope-walker whose steps seem to have constantly been protected by Fortune. His climb to power was hard. Suspect as the protégé of the Roman Mark Antony, Herod was first looked on with suspicious eyes by the Jews, but he managed to gain their approval thanks to the help of Pharisees, whose leaders, Samaias and Pollion, spoke up for him out of gratitude for sparing their lives when Herod took revenge on the judges of the Sanhedrin who had tried him in Galilee. The clever king also succeeded in softening the opposition of the pro-Hasmonaean Sadducee upper classes, for whom he was no more than a 'half-Jew', by marrying the Jewish princess Mariamme, the granddaughter of the ethnarch and high priest Hyrcanus II. In addition to the Pharisees and Sadducees, Herod was also on good terms with the Essenes, a by then long-established community, first mentioned in Josephus in mid-second century BCE. They owed this favourable treatment to the prophecy of the Essene Menahem who foretold Herod's elevation to the kingship of Judaea. With the death of Antigonus and Hyrcanus II, the Hasmonaean hereditary pontificate came to an end and Herod, being the secular head of state, arrogated to himself the right to appoint and dismiss Jewish high priests. This right was granted in New Testament times to his grandsons, Agrippa I and Agrippa II, by the emperor, and exercised in the meantime by the Roman governors of Judaea between 6 and 41 CE.

To secure his position, Herod had to ensure friendly relations with Rome and overcome the continuing hostility of some members of the Hasmonaean family. Remaining on good terms with Mark Antony became rather tricky because of the influence of Cleopatra, the Egyptian queen, on Herod's patron. This *femme fatale*, first the lover and later the wife of Antony, had cast an envious eye on the Judaean kingdom. Herod succeeded in minimizing his territorial losses, only some coastal towns and the area of Jericho were annexed to Egypt, while briefly contemplating, but wisely abandoning, the idea of a love affair with Cleopatra which he thought might provide him with an opportunity to get rid of her. The deteriorating relationship between Antony and Octavian, the future Augustus, created a new dilemma for Herod, but with his customary good luck he contrived to gain first the trust and later the close friendship of Augustus.

His feud with the Hasmonaean royalty was harder to settle as it was kept alive by the continuous intrigues of the female members of the court led by the king's Idumaean mother Cyprus and his sister Salome on the one hand and, on the other, his Hasmonaean wife Mariamme, with whom he was passionately in love, and her mother Alexandra. The outcome was bloody for the Hasmonaeans. The long list of family members executed by Herod include his beloved wife Mariamme and her two sons, Alexander and Aristobulus; her brother, the young high priest Aristobulus III, drowned in an arranged swimming pool accident; Mariamme's mother and her old grandfather, the harmless former high priest Hyrcanus II. The king's sister Salome also used her brother's good services to get rid of three of her husbands, one of them Herod's own uncle. Nevertheless, shortly after the execution in 4 BCE of Antipater, Herod's eldest son by the first of his ten wives, Salome and her fourth husband frustrated the dying king's final mad murder project by setting free a large group of Jewish notables whom they had been instructed by Herod to assassinate on his death so as to guarantee widespread mourning at the moment of the royal funeral in 4 BCE.

Herod the Murderer, a suitable model for the man who stands behind the Gospel legend of the massacre of the innocents, was nonetheless also Herod the Great. His foreign policy was outstandingly successful despite the fluctuations of fortune in the Roman world, and he was quite often solicitous and generous towards his Jewish subjects too. He went so far as to introduce substantial tax cuts to help the national economy after the severe famine of 25 BCE! He was a great promoter of Greek culture and, above all, he excelled in grandiose building projects at home and abroad. Among his achievements with New Testament relevance should be mentioned the construction of the port and the city of Caesarea, named after Caesar Augustus, the seat of the Roman governors of Judaea in the first century CE where St Paul spent two years in prison. He restored the city of Samaria and renamed it *Sebaste,* again in honour of Augustus. He erected a pagan temple in Caesarea Philippi, the city where the apostle Peter was to confess the Messiahship of Jesus. But above all, his greatest architectural memorial was the rebuilding of the Jerusalem sanctuary, known as Herod's Temple, some of whose remains, especially the Western or Wailing Wall, still stand today.

The life of Jesus began in the closing years of the reign of Herod the Great; this is one of the few points on which the Infancy Gospels of Matthew and Luke agree. But the main events which happened during the final year of Jesus' career (29/30 CE) belong to the next period of Jewish history.

Herod Archelaus – Herod Antipas – Roman prefects (4 BCE–41 CE) – The Public Career and Death of Jesus (29/30 CE)

Jesus did not bring peace into his world. His early years coincided with quarrels about who would be the heir of Herod and with political turmoil caused by a series of uprisings. The succession, confused by contradictory wills of the dying king, was decided by Augustus: the realm was divided into three parts among the surviving sons of Herod with Archelaus being put in charge of Judaea, Idumaea and

Samaria (4 BCE– 6 CE), Antipas of Galilee (4 BCE–39 CE), and Philip of the territories north and east of Galilee (4 BCE–33/4 CE). None of them inherited the royal title. Archelaus was made an ethnarch and the other two were given the lower rank of tetrarch. But while the settlement was still in the making, the death of the strong ruler encouraged revolutionary forces to come into the open. The Peraean Simon, the giant shepherd, Athronges, and especially Judas' son Ezechias revolted, but they were soon overcome by the army of Archelaus and especially by the legions of Varus, the Roman governor of Syria, who after crushing the rebellion crucified 2,000 Jewish revolutionaries outside Jerusalem, thus foreshadowing the harsher times to come in the first century CE.

No doubt this same Judas from Gamala, nicknamed Judas the Galilean, raised again the flag of rebellion in 6 CE, when as a preliminary to the annexation of Judaea as a Roman province after Archelaus's dismissal, Quirinius, the governor of Syria, organized a property registration with a view to reassessing taxes. This is the census of 6 CE, the date of which is clearly stated by the Jewish historian Josephus. Quirinius's census is the event that the Gospel of Luke wrongly places to the reign of Herod the Great in association with the legendary journey of the parents of Jesus, Joseph and Mary, from Nazareth to Bethlehem. The uprising of Judas the Galilean petered out, but the Zealot movement, which he launched in association with a Pharisee called Zadok, persisted throughout the next 60 years; it was responsible for most of the subsequent political unrest among Jews, and culminated in the catastrophic war, which between 66 and 70 CE devastated the country and destroyed Jerusalem together with all the Jewish state institutions. The eschatological discourse attributed to Jesus in the Synoptic Gospels (Mark 13; Matt. 24; Luke 21) is the echo of those dreadful events.

In 6 CE the political landscape of Palestine underwent a marked change. Galilee, where Jesus was growing up, continued its apparent political independence. As long as its ruler Herod Antipas maintained peace and paid his tribute to the emperor, he was allowed to rule unmolested. In Judaea, by contrast, after the deposition and banishment of Archelaus the government of the country was transferred to a Roman prefect, appointed by the emperor.

Rome in general preferred to delegate administrative power (the keeping of the peace and the collection of taxes) to the Jewish ruling classes, the chief priests and the Sanhedrin. Rome also abstained from direct interference with Jewish religious life. Indirectly the extensive powers of Roman governors included the appointment and dismissal of Jewish high priests. Most of them remained in office only for a short period, one year or a couple of years, with the exception of two, both of whom played an important part in the trial of Jesus: the former high priest Annas (6–15 CE) and his son-in-law Joseph Caiaphas, who sat on the pontifical throne from 18 to 36/7 CE. Annas interrogated Jesus and Caiaphas delivered him to Pilate. The Roman governors kept also the vestments of the high priest under their custody and thereby controlled the functions, which required the wearing of certain ceremonial robes. The Pharisee teachers, mostly active in Jerusalem and in the Judaean cities, enjoyed full freedom. Three famous masters, Hillel, some of whose ideas are reflected in the teaching of Jesus, Shammai, Hillel's opposite number, and Gamaliel the Elder, who is mentioned with approval in the Acts of the Apostles, flourished during the life time of Jesus in the early decades of the first century CE. There is no doubt that the ascetic Essenes, described by the writers Philo of Alexandria and Josephus, and represented by the sectarian Dead Sea Scrolls, were pursuing their reclusive religious existence at Qumran and elsewhere. They influenced Jewish life more by their fame and moral authority than by direct impact: the instruction of non-members was forbidden by their rules. Nevertheless their community may have served as a model for the organization of the first Christian church in Jerusalem, which like the Essene sect described by Josephus, Philo, Pliny the Elder and the Community Rule of Qumran, lived out of a common kitty administered by the apostles. Some of the charismatic rain makers and healers-exorcists like the grandsons of Honi, Abba Hilkiah and Hanan, and the Galilean man of God Hanina ben Dosa, also belonged to the same century, and lived in the period preceding the first Jewish war.

The public activity of Jesus neatly fits into the reign of the emperor Tiberius (14–37 CE). It occurred during the governorship of Pontius Pilate (26–36 CE) and the high priesthood of Caiaphas (18–36/7 CE). According to Luke, John the Baptist appeared on the scene in the fifteenth year of Tiberius (29 CE), and was soon followed by Jesus. Of the two great Jewish authors of the first century CE, Philo (20 BCE–40 CE) was Jesus' contemporary and Flavius Josephus (37–c. 100 CE) belonged to the next generation, which witnessed the beginnings of the Jewish-Christian community. The information about John the Baptist and Jesus contained in the *Jewish Antiquities* of Flavius Josephus, which sometimes does, and sometimes does not tally with the story contained in the Gospels, is judged authentic by the best scholarly opinion of today.

By the end of this period (41 CE), Augustus and Tiberius were already gone, but the insane Gaius Caligula was still there to make a nuisance of himself in Jewish affairs by insisting that his statue be installed in the Temple of Jerusalem and that he should be venerated as a god. Herod Antipas and Pontius Pilate were simultaneously sacked by the Romans and sent to exile in southern France. Caiaphas was also removed from the high priesthood. The leadership of the Christian movement in Judaea was in the hands of Peter and James the brother of the Lord, soon to be dominated outside the Land of Israel by the towering figure of Saul of Tarsus, St Paul. The Jesus movement was still rooted in Palestinian Jewish society, but was almost ready for a unilateral declaration of independence and for devoting itself to the evangelization of the Gentile world in the Roman Empire.

Agrippa I – Roman Procurators – First Rebellion (41–73/4 CE) – The Beginnings of Judaeo-Christianity and Career of St Paul

The period from the Agrippa I, the grandson of Herod the Great who was appointed king of the Jews by Caligula in 41 CE to the fall of Jerusalem and Masada at the end of the first war against the Romans (66–73/4 CE) attests a steadily worsening political situation. The Roman procurators in charge of the Jewish state from the death of Agrippa I in 44 CE until the outbreak of the rebellion in 66 CE were rarely able to exercise full control. Nor was the expert and willing help offered by Agrippa II, the son of Agrippa I, the reformed playboy of Roman high society, to whom the emperor Claudius assigned the kingdom of Gaulanitis, Batanaea and Trachonitis, sufficient to resolve the troubles. The murderous faction of Jewish revolutionaries known as *Sicarii* (dagger-men) made life impossible. They remained unaffected by the example made of two of the sons of Judas the Galilean whom Tiberius Julius Alexander, Roman governor of Judaea, caught and sentenced to crucifixion. The incompetent and corrupt last procurators further aggravated matters.

Nascent Christianity, too, had its ups and downs during those years. In Judaea two leading figures of the Palestinian church met with violent death. For reasons untold by the author of the Acts, the otherwise notoriously mild Agrippa I is said to have condemned James the son of Zebedee to decapitation, a secular form of death penalty no doubt for a secular crime, and the high priest Ananus, son of Ananus, ordered – unjustly according to Josephus – the execution by stoning of the saintly James, the brother of the Lord for having 'transgressed the law'. Church tradition places the martyrdom of the apostles Peter and Paul to the final years of Nero, whose reign ended in 68 CE. On the positive side the preaching of the gospel to Palestinian Jews continued, though without spectacular progress, but the decision of the council of the apostles in Jerusalem in 49 CE gave the green light to Paul and Barnabas for their remarkably efficacious mission among the Gentiles of the diaspora once the precondition of the acceptance of Judaism was cancelled and non-Jewish men could be baptized without being obliged first to undergo circumcision. Paul and his helpers were proclaiming the gospel among the inhabitants of Asia Minor and mainland Greece between 49 and 58 CE and the Pauline letters were all written in the fifties and possibly in the early sixties of the first century CE. Events of Paul's career neatly fit into Roman history. His appearance before the tribunal of Gallio, the brother of the philosopher Seneca, took place in Corinth between 51 and 53 CE, while Gallio was proconsul of Achaia, and Paul was arrested in Jerusalem in the closing years of the procuratorship of Felix (52–60 CE). As he was still a prisoner in

Caesarea two years later when Festus replaced Felix in 60 CE, his captivity must have begun in 58 CE. He was transferred to Rome for trial before Nero after surviving a shipwreck close to Malta at the end of 60 CE.

The storm clouds were gathering and despite the initial efforts of the Jewish upper classes the catastrophic war against the Roman Empire became inevitable. We know all the details from Josephus who at the beginning was himself a half-hearted leader of the revolt. Soon the command passed to men of violence, like John of Gischala and Simon bar Giora, and the most stubborn among them the captain of Masada, Eleazar son of Jairus, the grandson of the revolutionary patriarch, Judas the Galilean. But they were no match for the Roman forces of two future emperors, Vespasian and Titus. The fight was bloody. Captured Jews were crucified daily by their hundreds. The city was destroyed and the Temple reduced to ashes. Not even the seemingly impregnable stronghold of Masada could stop the men and the war machines of the Roman governor Silva in 73/4 CE. The discerning defenders preferred self-inflicted death to Roman torture and crucifixion.

According to Jewish tradition Yohanan ben Zakkai and Rabban Gamaliel settled, with Vespasian's permission, in the coastal town of Jamnia or Yavneh and, surrounded by a dedicated group of rabbis, set out to redefine, and thus save, a Jewish religion without Temple, high priest and Sanhedrin.

The state of the Jewish-Christian church is sketched in the eschatological discourse of Jesus in the Synoptic Gospels. Christian theological tradition, recorded centuries later by the historian Eusebius, interpreted the ruin of Jerusalem as divine punishment visited on the Jews 'for their abominable crimes against Christ and his apostles'. Eusebius further asserts that the members of the Jerusalem church, warned by a prophetic oracle before the outbreak of the war, migrated from the capital and settled in the town of Pella in Transjordan. We lack external support for his statement. Neither are we told about the future fate of those who had migrated to Pella although another Christian legend, referring to the persecution of the church by the leader of the second Jewish rebellion, Simeon bar Kosiba or Bar Kokhba, implies that

15

the refugees of Pella re-crossed the Jordan after the end of the war and settled again in the Land of Israel.

From the Fall of Jerusalem to the End of the Rebellion under Hadrian – The Departure of Christianity from its Jewish Social Setting (70–135 CE)

The aftermath of the first failed rebellion against Rome brought hardship to both Jews and Christians. The victorious emperor Vespasian treated the whole conquered territory as his private property and in addition to the loss of the national and religious institutions, all the Jews in Palestine and the diaspora were subjected to the humiliation of having the annual poll tax, which they willingly paid for the upkeep of the Jerusalem sanctuary, confiscated and converted to a yearly tribute, known as *fiscus Iudaicus* or Jewish tax, which was to support of the temple of Jupiter Capitolinus in Rome. It was collected with particular harshness under Domitian (81–96 CE), though apparently the severity was relaxed according to a coin minted by his successor, the emperor Nerva (96–8 CE). Conversion to Judaism, considered as the adoption of atheism, was also strictly prohibited. The rebellion of the Jews in Egypt and Cyrene in 115 CE under Trajan added further fuel to the virulent anti-Judaism of the Romans and the major conflict of the second war (132–5 CE) was already looming on the horizon.

The causes of the Jewish uprising inspired and led by Simeon bar Kosiba or Bar Kokhba during the reign of Hadrian have long been a subject of debate, but the circumstances of the war and the revolutionary administration of the country have become better known now thanks to the archives of legal documents and letters discovered in the caves of Wadi Murabbaat and Wadi Seiyal in the Judaean desert in the 1950s and early 1960s. The Roman governor of Judaea, Tineius Rufus, was unable to stand up to the guerrilla forces of Simeon, the self-proclaimed imperious head of state – he called himself Prince (*Nasi*) of Israel – and it took three years of strenuous struggle with much blood shed on both sides before Julius Severus, the greatest general of Rome urgently summoned from far-distant Britain, managed to quell the revolt in 135 CE.

16

For years persecution reigned, famous rabbis, among them Akiba, lost their lives and the practice of the Jewish religion was prohibited under the pain of death. Jews in droves were expelled from Judaea and their ancient capital, lavishly rebuilt by the emperor as a pagan city, was even deprived of its name and became *Aelia* in honour of the triumphant Publius *Aelius* Hadrianus. But outside Judaea, and especially in Galilee, Jewish life continued and thanks to the zeal and persistence of the rabbinic leaders Jewish religion, re-codified in the Mishnah and the Palestinian or more exactly Galilean Talmud, gained a new lease of life.

The Palestinian Jewish members of the Jesus movement, a small Judaean sect in Roman eyes, continued to exist after the destruction of Jerusalem. Church fathers refer to them as Ebionites or Nazoraeans. They were treated as heretics for resisting the developed Christian doctrines of the divinity of Jesus and his virginal conception, and strictly observing the traditional Jewish way of life. Little evidence has survived concerning them, but occasional anecdotes preserved in rabbinic literature, such as the offer of the Jewish-Christian Jacob of Kefar Sekhaniah to heal a rabbi in the name of Jesus and the legendary admission of the noted Rabbi Eliezer ben Hyrcanus of having accepted a teaching of Jesus suggest that the two groups were still on rather unfriendly speaking terms.

If Christian tradition handed down in the fourth century by Eusebius can be trusted, Roman search for Jewish revolutionaries from the time of Vespasian until Trajan affected also the family of Jesus, suspected of propagating hopes in the return of the Messiah. No doubt the cooling down of the expectation of an imminent Second Coming soon removed the threat of Roman retaliation, though not before the grandsons of Jude, the grandnephews of Jesus, were put on a political blacklist under Domitian and Symeon son of Clopas, the cousin of Jesus and the successor of James the brother of the Lord as bishop of Jerusalem suffered a martyr's death under Trajan in the first decade of the second century CE.

The outlook for the non-Jewish Christians of the churches founded by Paul in the Roman world was equally gloomy. Already under Nero they were seen as members of a pernicious superstition and many of them were crucified in Rome and, while membership of the church was not held to be a sufficient ground for prosecution under Trajan, it carried a *prima facie* suspicion of criminality. In the course of the two centuries following the defeat of Bar Kokhba the situation of the Jews in the Roman Empire quietly improved while that of the Christians subject to successive persecutions, if anything, worsened. However, the victory of the emperor Constantine at the Milvian Bridge in 312 CE reversed the process and gave Christianity the upper hand.

This survey of Jewish and Judaeo-Christian history in a nutshell from the annexation of Judaea as a Roman province in 63 BCE to the end of the second Jewish rebellion against Rome in 135 CE, and the *Who's Who* itself, are intended to advance a dynamic understanding of Jesus in his time. He stands in the middle of 200 eventful years: he died roughly 100 years after Pompey's entry into Jerusalem and 100 years before the defeat of Bar Kokhba at the battle of Bether.

It is my sincere hope that the historical perspective opened up through these vignettes will enable the reader to grasp the historical reality of the leading figures of the New Testament and to understand better their link with the Jewish and Roman protagonists of the society of their age.

Note

1 Geza Vermes, 2006, *Who's Who in the Age of Jesus*, London: Penguin.

2

Jesus the Jew

When I had the honour of being the cast-away on Sue Lawley's *Desert Island Discs* on Radio 4, she introduced me as the author of *Jesus the Jew*,[1] a book which, to quote her words, I 'wrote for fun'. The more exact truth is that around 1970 I decided, after years of hard labour on a history of the Jews in the age of Jesus, to do something enjoyable and use the technical expertise acquired in preparing the history volumes for approaching the figure of Jesus from the vantage point of the Judaism of his time.

Jesus the Jew, which has now become an SCM Classic, was not the fruit of subjective religious preoccupations, but of detached scholarly concerns. Its writing was prompted – as I stated in the preface to the first edition – by a single-minded search for fact and reality undertaken out of feeling for the tragedy of Jesus of Nazareth, distorted by Christian and Jewish myth alike. The book made an impact and can now be read, in addition to the original English, in seven languages, and an eighth translation into Polish is in the making under the auspices of a publishing house which is also responsible for bringing out several of the previous Pope's writings! What John Paul II would have thought of it, I prefer not to speculate on.

First published in 1973, *Jesus the Jew* was followed at ten-year intervals by *Jesus and the World of Judaism*[2] and *The Religion of Jesus the Jew*,[3] both by SCM Press. In 2000 another volume was issued by Penguin entitled *The Changing Faces of Jesus*.[4] Those who wish to know the inside story of my work on Jesus will find the essentials, as well as some amusing tit-bits, in *Providential Accidents*,[5] my autobiography which saw the light of day in 1998.

As for future plans, readers of the literary gossip column of the *Daily Telegraph* may have come across the following snippet on 24 February last: 'Geza Vermes, author of several other books on Jesus, is preparing another manuscript. "My publishers told me that I am free to choose any subject provided that I put the word Jesus in the title",' he says with a shrug of the shoulders. The columnist then added, 'A senior executive at Penguin whom I asked about it confided cheerfully: "We are trying to get him write one just called Christ!, but he won't wear it."' So, though not under that short title, work is proceeding.

After these preliminaries, all that remains for me is to present in a nutshell what we know about the historical Jesus, Jesus the Jew.

The New Testament, which is our chief source, contains two very different pictures. For the author of the Gospel of John, who wrote at the beginning of the second century, Jesus was a heavenly being who in time became incarnate and briefly took up residence among men before returning to heaven. For Saint Paul, on the other hand, he was the universal saviour of mankind whose impending triumphant return was eagerly awaited by Paul and by the first Christians.

Against these majestic portraits stands the Jesus of the Synoptic Gospels. Mark, Matthew and Luke were written between 70 and 100 CE, but reflect considerably older traditions. These Gospels do not depict him as divine; on the contrary, he is even quoted there as objecting to be called good because only God is good. This very human person, who is the subject of *Jesus the Jew*, was a carpenter in the village of Nazareth. He lived with his parents, Joseph and Mary, his four brothers, James, Joseph, Judas and Simon, and his several sisters in the Galilee governed by Antipas, son of king Herod the Great (d. 4 BCE).

What can a historian say about Jesus? The main body of the story relating to him is recorded in Mark, the earliest of the Gospels. It includes no introduction dealing with the birth of Jesus, nor a conclusion recounting the apparitions following the death of Christ, as do Matthew and Luke. Mark begins with the public career of Jesus, and is silent on his childhood, youth, and early manhood. We learn nothing about his education. When Jesus began to teach, people apparently wondered how this untrained man had acquired such wisdom.

We are nowhere told that Jesus was married. Celibate life was unusual among Jews, except among the monkish Essenes described by Flavius Josephus and the Dead Sea Scrolls. Yet the Gospels contain no hint that Jesus was an Essene; indeed his religious outlook contradicts theirs. His choice for the unmarried state may have been motivated by his conviction that he was a prophet, a vocation which demanded total renunciation of worldly pleasures to ensure incessant spiritual alertness.

Jesus emerged from 30 years of obscurity when he answered John the Baptizer's appeal to baptism and repentance. He remained in his company until John was imprisoned by Herod Antipas. Jesus then decided to continue John's mission in Galilee. He called for repentance and proclaimed the imminent arrival of the Kingdom of God, symbolizing a new age in which God would rule unopposed by forces of darkness. He preached in village synagogues by the Lake of Galilee, and accompanied his teaching with charismatic acts of healing and exorcism. He was known as 'the prophet Jesus from Nazareth in Galilee'.

Jesus was a captivating teacher and attracted to himself 12 apostles, largely from among the local fishermen, and a small group of close disciples. During his itinerant ministry he hardly ever left Galilee, venturing no farther than the close-by districts of Tyre and Sidon (in present-day Lebanon), Caesarea Philippi (in Syria), and the territory of the pagan cities of the Greek Decapolis, mostly in Jordan. In his heart he was a countryman who felt at home in villages, vineyards and orchards, and in the cornfields where lilies grew. He shunned cities. He is never said to have set foot in Sepphoris, the capital of Galilee only a few miles distant from his own Nazareth. The first three Gospels bring him only once to Jerusalem from where he did not return.

His teaching struck the audience as new because of his emphasis on the deep religious significance and permanent validity of the Law of Moses, and because his teaching style was different from that of synagogue preachers. Unlike these scribes, Jesus felt no need to produce biblical proof texts to support his message. His spiritual authority was revealed instead by his deeds, the curing of the sick and the possessed.

The contemporaries of Jesus held evil spirits responsible for illness and sin. What for them was demonic possession is called today nervous, mental or psychosomatic disease. For instance the young deaf-mute whom Jesus was to exorcize is characterized as having the symptoms of an epileptic fit: convulsion, falling to the ground, rolling about, and foaming at the mouth. For Jesus, and not just for him, healing, expelling demons and forgiving sins were synonyms. The Dead Sea Scrolls also allude to a Jewish exorcist who cured a Babylonian king from a long illness by forgiving his sins.

Jesus usually healed by touch and exorcized by verbal command. Neither of these actions amounted to 'work' which might have legitimately been construed as a breach of the Sabbath. Only narrow-minded village lawyers could accuse him of breaking the law of sabbatical rest.

Jesus was not the only charismatic of his age. Some of his fellow saints, the righteous Honi and the much sought-after Galilean healer Hanina ben Dosa, were also famous for their miraculous powers. They were reputed to have brought rain and prevented famine, cured the sick and kept the demons under control. Like Jesus, they were revered as latter-day prophet Elijahs. In sum, Jesus fitted well into the spiritual landscape of first-century Palestine. The uncommitted Jewish historian Flavius Josephus depicted Jesus about the end of the first century CE as a wise man and a performer of astonishing deeds. For his own followers, Jesus was 'a man attested by God with mighty works and wonders' as the Acts of the Apostles informs us.

What distinguished Jesus from the other holy men of his time was the simple beauty and magnetism of his message. He was not a philosopher and had no liking for abstract ideas. He proclaimed the imminence of the Kingdom of God. He never defined the Kingdom but rather likened it to the rich harvest, or to the tiny mustard seed which mysteriously grew into a tall shrub, or to the leaven which imperceptibly turned flour into bread. All these

similitudes hint at a new God-centred world to which Jesus prepared the way. He was convinced that the impending presence of
this new reality was signalled by his charismatic activity. Echoing
Isaiah, he declared that if the blind see, the lame walk, the lepers
are cleansed, the deaf hear and the dead re-awaken, then the Day
of the Lord is on the doorstep and the Kingdom of God is at hand.
The Dead Sea Scrolls also envisage the age of the Messiah as a
time when the captives go free, the blind recover their sight, the
bent are straightened, the sick healed, and the dead revived.

Jesus was clear about the duties of his followers wishing to enter the Kingdom. Repentance, trust and child-like simplicity had
to come first, followed by total devotion and a readiness to surrender at once oneself and all one's possessions for the sake of the
Kingdom. The present had to overshadow the future. Forward
planning was meaningless: the time of this world and of its institutions could easily run out before tomorrow.

The religion of Jesus was one of urgency, enthusiasm, compassion and love. If he had any preference, it was for the little ones
and the despised. In his view, the return of a single lost sheep, a
tax-collector or a harlot would cause more rejoicing in heaven
than the secure progress of 99 righteous ones.

Since the charismatic deeds of Jesus were seen as the signs of
the messianic age, it is not surprising that many expected him to
reveal himself as the Messiah, the divinely appointed king who
would defeat the Romans and establish justice and peace on
earth. The first three Gospels suggest that Jesus was not keen on
being proclaimed the Christ. He had no political ambitions. Apart
from a couple of doubtful passages, he declined to give a straight
answer to the question, Are you the Messiah? His usual reply was
evasive, like 'You have said so', or 'You say that I am', implying
the tacit 'but not I'.

Rumours that nevertheless he might be the Messiah undoubt-
edly contributed to his downfall, but his tragic end was precipitated by an unfortunate episode in the Temple of Jerusalem. The
noisy business transacted by the merchants and money-changers
in the courtyard of the house of God outraged Jesus and the in-
dignant rural holy man overturned their tables and threw them

out. He thus created a fracas in the overcrowded city in the days leading up to Passover when the Jews expected the Messiah to arrive. So Jesus appeared to the Jewish and Roman authorities as a potential threat to law and order. The authorities had to act promptly and they did so, though the Jewish leaders preferred to pass the responsibility to Pontius Pilate. In short, Jesus died on the Roman cross because he did the wrong thing in the wrong place at the wrong time.

However, Jesus made such a profound impact on the mind of his apostles and disciples that they attributed to the power of his name the continued efficacy of their charismatic healing activity and their preaching. Crucified, dead and buried, Jesus rose in the hearts of his disciples who loved him, and so he lived on.

Notes

1 Geza Vermes, 1973, *Jesus the Jew*, London: SCM Press.
2 Geza Vermes, 1983, *Jesus and the World of Judaism*, London: SCM Press.
3 Geza Vermes, 1993, *The Religion of Jesus the Jew*, London: SCM Press.
4 Geza Vermes, 2000, *The Changing Faces of Jesus*, London: Penguin.
5 Geza Vermes, 1998, *Providential Accidents*, London: SCM Press.

3

The Changing Faces of Jesus in the New Testament and Since

According to an oft-repeated saying, books on Jesus tell more about their authors than about Jesus himself. I would like to dissent or at least to claim that my case is an exception. If justification is needed, it may be found in my autobiography, *Providential Accidents*.[1] In a nutshell, my interest in Jesus was not the product of my religious toing and froing. I was born in an assimilated and religiously detached Hungarian Jewish family. At the age of six, together with my parents, I was baptized Roman Catholic and remained in that church as a student, a seminarian, the member of the religious order of Notre Dame de Sion and for six years as a priest, until I reached the age of 32 years. Then followed a period of groping at the end of which, by the late 1960s, I found myself quietly, without a spiritual storm, back at my Jewish roots. But my fascination with the figure of Jesus was not the fruit of these wanderings. If personal experience had anything to do with my way of understanding Jesus, it can be located in an insider's knowledge of both Christianity and Judaism.

During my student days at Louvain in Belgium I was never attracted to the New Testament. My teachers were too theological for my liking. My enthusiasm was first focused on the Hebrew Old Testament, and afterwards on the then newly discovered Dead Sea Scrolls which have kept me busy throughout my whole academic life. My doctoral dissertation discussed the historical framework of Qumran and was published in French in 1953.[2] A translation of the Scrolls into English followed in 1962;[3] the original booklet of 250 pages has grown over the years into a volume of close to 700 pages.[4] The Scrolls led me to a study of ancient Jewish Bible interpretation, and there for the first time I had to pay serious attention to the treatment of the Old Testament in the New.[5] From the mid-1960s I found myself involved in a 20-year-long collective labour aimed at revising, enlarging and rewriting a nineteenth-century modern classic, *The History of the Jewish People in the Age of Jesus Christ* by Emil Schürer.[6] After completing the first of the three volumes of this gigantic monument, I decided to take a little time off, relax and enjoy myself by using the historical knowledge freshly gained for a new approach to the Gospel account of Jesus. To be more precise, I wanted to plunge the New Testament into the sea of the Judaism of its age in order to discover what the figure of Jesus might look like when perceived, not through the distorting lens of 2,000 years of evolving Christian belief and theology, but through the eyes, ears and mentality of Jesus' own Jewish contemporaries. Out of this endeavour emerged in 1973 *Jesus the Jew*,[7] intended to describe what kind of person Jesus was. The book made an impact and was followed at ten yearly intervals by *Jesus and the World of Judaism*,[8] sketching the message of the Gospels, and *The Religion of Jesus the Jew*,[9] a full-scale endeavour to portray Jesus as a religious man.

The Changing Faces of Jesus[10] has much in common with and often relies on the trilogy which preceded it, yet it also greatly differs from it. The approach is broader: instead of depending only on the first three Gospels which are considered closest to historical reality, it investigates also the Gospel of John, the letters of Paul and the rest of the New Testament. Moreover, it is addressed to a wider readership and in particular has a different scenario. In the trilogy the inquiry was essentially historical; here it is both literary and historical. The purpose of *The Changing Faces of Jesus* is to sketch four different portraits in the various levels of New Testament literature before trying to guess the fifth one lying beneath the earliest layer of Gospel tradition.

The arrangement of the portraits follows their degree of sophistication rather than a strictly chronological line. I begin with the Gospel of John, the Everest of New Testament Christology, a Gospel which happens to be not only the most advanced, but also the latest New Testament representation of Christ, dating to the opening years of the second century CE. John fundamentally departs from the earlier Synoptic Gospels of Matthew, Mark and Luke in its religious outlook. Its story telling, too, has little in common with the Synoptics with the exception of the section leading to the crucifixion and death of Jesus. John's Gospel largely ignores Jesus' teaching about the Kingdom of God, and replaces the pithy proverbs and vivid, God-centred parables of the Jesus of the Synoptics with long, rambling speeches in which Jesus continuously reflects on himself. In the Fourth Gospel we encounter not a real, flesh and blood Galilean charismatic, but a stranger from heaven, temporarily exiled on earth, who is longing to return to his celestial home. The 252 brilliantly chosen Greek words of the Prologue offer a pellucid abstract of John's Gospel, the summit of New Testament theology. The eternal and divine Word of God, who took part in the creation of the world, became incarnate in time to reveal to men the face of the invisible God.

The Johannine portrait of Jesus foreshadows and epitomizes later Christianity, as we know it. The great doctrinal controversies of the church in the first millennium of its history mostly revolved around ideas first mooted in the Fourth Gospel. The orthodox doctrine relating to Christology – the one person and two natures of Jesus Christ – and to the Holy Trinity, all spring from the spiritual Gospel of John. John is the father of the theology of eastern Christianity.

Here ends my synopsis of the first two chapters of the *Changing Faces*, dealing with John. The next two are devoted to the high peaks of the teaching of St Paul.

The letters of Paul chronologically precede John by half a century, but from the point of view of doctrinal development stand only a little below him. As is well known, Paul is held by many to be the true founder of the church and the chief inspiration of the atonement-redemption theology of western Christianity. Closing his eyes to the earthly Jesus whom he never met, and about whom he had nothing original to report, Paul's gaze was fixed on Christ, the universal Saviour of both Jews and of non-Jews. This superhuman, but not quite divine Christ, reminiscent of the heroes of the mystery religions then so popular in the Graeco-Roman world, played the ultimate lead part in a cosmic drama of redemption. Adam, the first man, left death and sinfulness to posterity, but the last Adam (Jesus Christ) brought to all forgiveness, life and salvation. Paul's astonishing success in the non-Jewish world, contrasted with the failure of the early Christian mission among Jews, was itself part of this mystery play. The Second Coming of Jesus, fervently expected by Paul and the primitive church, could not happen – he thought – before the gospel had reached all the Gentile nations. He also imagined that its progress among the heathen would kindle the jealousy of the Jews who would not suffer passively the takeover of their spiritual patrimony by non-Jews. And once the Jews decided to enter the race, they would advance by leaps and bounds and soon catch up with, and overtake the leaders. Thus the whole of mankind, both Jews and Gentiles, would enjoy the salvation mediated through Christ.

Paul believed that he himself was commissioned by God to preach Christ to all the nations on the eastern and northern shore of the Mediterranean Sea, starting with Syria, Asia Minor, and Greece. He then planned to travel to Rome and convert Italy, and finally rush to Spain. No doubt, it was in Spain, at the westernmost extremity of the inhabited universe, that Paul expected to hear the trumpet signalling the day of Christ's return, hailed by the mixed alleluia chorus of Gentiles and Jews.

As is often the case with beautiful dreams, they end before their climax is reached. Paul never arrived in Spain. Jews and Christians are still divided, and two millennia have passed without the Second Coming. But Christianity still endures, and this is largely due to the spiritual vision of Jesus sketched by the odd-man-out among the apostles who never saw him in the flesh.

This takes us to the third portrait of Jesus, the one contained in the first half of the Acts of the Apostles: the Jesus seen and preached by Palestinian Jewish Christianity. It is far distant from John's mystical vision of the divine Christ and from Paul's mystery drama of salvation. The Jesus of the Acts is a Galilean charismatic character, elevated by God to the dignity of Lord and Messiah after raising him from the dead. Instead of considering Jesus as God or a temporary expatriate from heaven, according to the Acts (2.22), Peter qualifies him in his first christological

28

statement proclaimed to a crowd in Jerusalem as 'a man attested . . . by God with mighty works and wonders and signs', that is to say a Jewish prophet.

Stepping further back, at least as far as the nature of the tradition transmitted by them is concerned, we encounter in chapter 6 the Jesus of the Synoptic Gospels of Mark, Matthew and Luke. He is depicted as still living and moving along the dusty and rocky paths of rural Galilee and comes onstage as an itinerant healer, exorcist and preacher, admired by the simple folk, the sick and the social outcasts – the sinners, the prostitutes and the tax-collectors – but cause of scandal and annoyance to the *petit bourgeois* village scribes and synagogue presidents. His sympathizers venerated him as a miracle-working prophet and from an early stage, though apparently without his encouragement, his name began to be linked to that of the Messiah, son of David. His beneficial charismatic actions were seen as representing the portents of the messianic age in which the blind see, the deaf hear, the lame walk and the lepers are cleansed. He was not a revolutionary, and entertained no political ambition. The main subject of his proclamation was the imminent arrival of a new regime, and he saw himself as the person entrusted by the Father, whom he loved and worshipped, to lead the Jews through the gate of repentance into the spiritual promised land. 'Repent for the Kingdom of God is at hand!'

He fell foul of the high-priestly authorities in a politically unstable Jerusalem because he did the wrong thing in the wrong place at the wrong time. The wrong thing was the disturbance which Jesus caused by overturning the stalls and tables of the merchants of sacrificial animals and the money-changers who sold the correct silver coins prescribed for gifts to the sanctuary. The wrong place was the Temple of Jerusalem where large crowds of locals and pilgrims foregathered and formed a potential hotbed for explosive revolutionary activity. And the days leading to Passover, the feast of Liberation and the expected date of the manifestation of the Messiah, was the worst possible time because at that very tense moment the nerves of the guardians of law and order reached breaking point. Hence the tragedy of Jesus. Seen as a potential threat to peace, he was arrested by the Jewish leaders who, however, preferred not to take the responsibility for his death on themselves and handed him over to the secular power. So Jesus was executed on a Roman cross by the notoriously cruel governor of Judaea, Pontius Pilate.

This portrait painted by the Synoptics of a charismatic, messianic healer, exorcist and preacher of God's Kingdom is what one might call the gospel truth about Jesus. But this picture needs to be immersed into the real world of first-century Palestinian Judaism as it is known from the Dead Sea Scrolls, the works of the first century Jewish historian Flavius Josephus and the rest of post-biblical literature pre-rabbinic and rabbinic, works in which we encounter other prophetic-charismatic characters, albeit of lesser stature than Christ, such as Honi, Hanina ben Dosa or Jesus son of Ananias, with whom he can be compared. It is by looking through that prism that we may discover, concealed beneath the writings of Matthew, Mark and Luke, the shadowy face of the 'real' Jesus. I will not give away all the secrets of chapter 7 of *The Changing Faces* – you will have to read the book to discover them – but I will share with you my summation of the Jesus of history.

Here is the conclusion: the face of Jesus, truly human, wholly theocentric, passionately faith-inspired and under the imperative impulse of the here and now, impressed itself so deeply on the minds of his disciples that not even the shattering blow of the cross could arrest its continued real presence. It compelled them to carry on in his name their mission as healers, exorcists and preachers of the Kingdom of God. It was only a generation or two later, with the increasing delay of the Second Coming, that the image of the Jesus familiar from experience began to fade, covered over first by the theological and mystical dreamings of Paul and John, and afterwards by the dogmatic speculations of church-centred Gentile Christianity.

By the end of the first century, Christianity had lost sight of the real Jesus and of the original meaning of his message. Paul, John and their churches replaced him by the Christ of faith. The swiftness of the obliteration was due to a premature change in cultural perspective. Within decades the message of the historical Jesus was transferred from its Aramaic-Hebrew linguistic context, from its Galilean-Palestinian geographical setting, and its Jewish religious framework to the primarily Greek-speaking pagan Mediterranean world of classical cultural background. The change took place at too early a stage. The clay was still soft and malleable and could easily be moulded into any shape the potter cared to choose. As a result, the new church, by then mostly Gentile, soon lost awareness of being Jewish; indeed, it became progressively anti-Jewish.

Another twist exerted an adverse effect on the appeal of the Christian message to Palestinian and diaspora Jews. Jesus, the charismatic religious Jew, was metamorphosed into the transcendent object of the Christian faith. The Kingdom of God proclaimed by the fiery prophet from Nazareth did not mean much to the average new recruit from Alexandria, Antioch, Ephesus, Corinth or Rome. During the second and third centuries, the leading teachers of the church, trained in Greek philosophy, such as Irenaeus of Lyons, Clement, Origen and Athanasius of Alexandria, substituted for the existential manifesto of Jesus advocating repentance and submission to God a programme steeped in metaphysical speculation on the nature and person of the incarnate Word of God and on the mutual tie between the divine persons of the Most Holy Trinity. They could proceed freely since by that time there was no longer any Jewish voice in Christendom to sound the alarm.

It is of course true that if Christianity had not taken root in the provinces of the Roman Empire, it would have remained an insignificant Jewish sect with no external appeal. So when the early church decided that non-Jews could be admitted into the fold, it was logical to attempt a 'translation' of the Christian message for the benefit of the non-Jewish world. This inculturation or acculturation is valid provided it does not lead to substantial distortion. To avoid such distortion, it is necessary that the process of adaptation remains in the hands of the representatives of the home culture (Judaism in the present case). However, in the case of Christianity the inculturation was handled by Gentiles who were only superficially acquainted with the Jewish religion of Jesus. As a result, within a relatively short period no Jew was able to find acceptable the new incultured doctrines of Jesus presented by the church. In fact, I think Jesus himself would have failed to acknowledge it as his own.

Thereafter the growing anti-Judaism of the church further distanced Christian culture from the world of Jesus. At the beginning of the fifth century Saint Jerome, the only Hebrew expert of Christendom, compared the sound made by Jewish synagogue worshippers to the grunting of pigs and the braying of donkeys.[11] His contemporary, Saint John Chrysostom, bishop of Constantinople, referred to the synagogues of the Jewish Christ-killers as brothels, the citadel of the devil, and the abyss of perdition.[12] Later Christian anti-Semites, Luther among them, had such models to imitate. It is worth recording that Julius Streicher, the editor of the notorious Nazi journal, *Der Stürmer*, claimed in his defence before the Allies' tribunal that if he was guilty of anti-Semitism, so was Luther. His magazine simply repeated Luther's slogans.

As is well known the age-old religious anti-Semitism continued largely unabated until after the Second World War. Yet it is to be recognized that the Protestant reformation in the sixteenth century caused a considerable sea change. The reformers, inspired by the spirit of the Renaissance, resurrected the Bible and proclaimed the Hebrew Old Testament and the Greek New Testament the ultimate sources of divine revelation. So the Protestant scholars and Scripture-reading believers were brought closer to the biblical religion, and indirectly closer to Jesus. Still under the impact of the ideals of the Renaissance, Protestant New Testament scholars began to interest themselves in post-biblical Jewish literature. The seventeenth-century renowned Cambridge divine John Lightfoot recommended to Christians the study of rabbinic literature.[13] The Talmud would be useful to them for a deeper understanding of the Gospels although it poisons the mind of the Jews!

The strange bed-fellowship of anti-Judaic attitude and expertise in Jewish studies continued in Christian circles until the middle of the last century. This is scandalously exemplified in the person of Gerhard Kittel, the editor of the classic ten-volume *Theologi-*

cal Dictionary of the New Testament[14] who was also a regular contributor to official German Nazi anti-Semitic publications. Only the realization of the horror of the Holocaust put this line of 'scholarship' beyond the pale.

By then New Testament criticism, begun in the eighteenth century, had made considerable progress and the discovery of many ancient Jewish documents, chief among them the Dead Sea Scrolls, further enriched the field of comparative study. Thus a new era opened in the quest for the original meaning of Christianity. During the last 30 years dozens of books on the historical Jesus began to sprout from every corner of the religious and non-religious scholarly world.

Since 1945 the perspective has changed to an almost unrecognizable extent. Today the Jewishness of Jesus is axiomatic whereas in 1973 the title of my book, *Jesus the Jew*, still shocked conservative Christians. To accept that Jesus was a Jew means not only that he was born into the Jewish people, but that his religion, his culture, his psychology, and his mode of thinking and teaching were all Jewish. Over the last 50 years, Christian and Jewish scholars have worked together and a significant dialogue has developed between enlightened Christians and Jews.

Jesus the Jew, the charismatic Hasid, meets today with growing recognition, and not just in academic circles or exclusively among professing Christians. With the arrival of the third millennium the time appears ripe for a concerted effort aimed at improving and refining our understanding of the real Jesus and the birth of the Christian movement that arose in his wake.

Notes

1 Geza Vermes, 1998, *Providential Accidents*, London: SCM Press and Lanham, MD: Rowman and Littlefield.

2 Geza Vermes, 1953, *Les manuscrits du désert de Juda*, Paris: Desclée.

3 Geza Vermes, 1962, *The Dead Sea Scrolls in English*, London: Penguin.

4 Geza Vermes, 1997, *The Complete Dead Sea Scrolls in English*, London: Penguin.

5 Geza Vermes, 1961, *Scripture and Tradition in Judaism*, Leiden: Brill.

6 Volumes I–III, Edinburgh: T. & T. Clark, 1973–1987.

7 Geza Vermes, 1973, *Jesus the Jew: A Historian's Reading of the Gospels*, London: Collins. Republished by SCM Press in 1983.

8 Geza Vermes, 1983, *Jesus and the World of Judaism*, London: SCM Press.

9 Geza Vermes, 1993, *The Religion of Jesus the Jew*, London: SCM Press.

10 Geza Vermes, 2001, *The Changing Faces of Jesus*, London: Penguin and New York: Viking Penguin.

11 *In Amos 5:23* (Patrologia Latina xxv, 1054).

12 *Homilia I* (Patrologia Graeca xlviii, 847).

13 *Horae Hebraicae et Talmudicae*, Leipzig, 1658–1675.

14 Gerhard Kittel, 1933–1976, *Theologisches Wörterbuch zum Neuen Testament*, Stuttgart: Kohlhammer.

4

Jesus: God in Spite of Himself

An Interview with the Parisian Magazine *Le Point*

The real Jesus was to begin with a healer and exorcist endowed with astonishing charismatic power. Devoted to the cause of God till his death, he intended first of all to regenerate Judaism.

What is known about Jesus?

Very little. His life is recounted in the four Gospels recorded between 40 and 80 years after his death. Some factual information has been handed down by later historians, the Jewish Josephus and the Roman Tacitus. One fact is clearly established: he was crucified under Pontius Pilate, prefect of Judaea between 26 and 36 CE. The Gospels describe Jesus as a Galilean who was active around the Lake of Gennesaret. According to Matthew and Luke he was born under the reign of Herod the Great who died in 4 BCE. With the exception of the anecdote of the 12 year-old Jesus teaching in the Temple, the Gospels say nothing about his childhood.

Do we know anything regarding his family and his social circumstances?

He was poor and unmarried. He lived for 30 years in the townlet of Nazareth with his parents, Joseph and Mary, his four brothers and at least two sisters. The Church, which has made a dogma out of the virginity of Mary, asserts that the siblings issued from an earlier marriage of Joseph, who was a widower. The oldest Gospels, the Synoptics (Mark, Matthew and Luke) allude to a tense relationship between Jesus and his family, including his mother. Mark and Matthew report that the family sought to discourage Jesus from accomplishing his mission. In a passage in the Synoptics Jesus rejects his mother and brothers when they tried to interrupt his teaching. The more recent Gospel of John presents a different scenario; Jesus is invited with his mother and brothers to a wedding in Cana. Mary reappears at the foot of the cross. However, the role attributed to her by the Church has nothing to do with the texts.

What was Jesus' education like?

He was a builder or a carpenter, but his vocabulary and the images he employs make one think rather of a countryman. The famous anecdote of the 12-year-old Jesus instructing the Scripture experts in the Temple is a later invention. Against the divinized picture which started to be formulated by the apostle Paul, Jesus was a simple and modest man. He was a prophet in the tradition of the prophets Elijah and Elisha of the Bible, who were also active in the northern area of Palestine. Like Elijah and Elisha, Jesus also was endowed with outstanding charismatic power. The Gospels act as witnesses: Jesus is a healer able to cure diseases (paralysis, blindness . . .), an exorcist who expels demons, a wonder worker. This was in no way extraordinary in those days: rabbinic literature refers to other known healers and Flavius Josephus speaks of Jesus as a 'wise man' and a 'performer of prodigies'.

When did Jesus start to preach?

The beginning of his public career coincided with the ministry of John the Baptist, which is dated by Luke to the 15th year of the reign of Tiberius, in 29 CE. According to Mark and Luke, when Jesus received baptism from John, a heavenly voice informed him that he was God's beloved son. Matthew and John advance that it was John the Baptist who heard the voice and announced the election of Jesus. The statements relative to the duration of his ministry are contradictory: in the Synoptics he was preaching only one year while John speaks of three Passover festivals, which imply about three years. Later Church tradition is based on John.

Who formed the audience of Jesus?

The Gospels claim that he recruited 12 apostles and 70 disciples who were to help him with his mission. As an itinerant preacher, he delivered his message in the streets, in various places, on the shore of the lake. Straightaway he encountered much success. The crowds greeted him as 'the prophet from Nazareth'. It is important to note that only the Gospel of John accuses the Jewish people and the chief priests of having plotted his death before the last (and according to the Synoptics, the unique) visit of Jesus to Jerusalem.

What was Jesus' message?

Jesus was an eschatological prophet who proclaimed the arrival of the Kingdom of God in the near future, as it were tomorrow. Hence he demanded a total devotion to the cause of God, a renunciation by the faithful of all material possessions and even the abandonment of their families. It is to be underlined that this appeal was addressed only to the Jewish people, the 'lost sheep of the house of Israel'. The texts are clear: the apostles of Jesus were ordered not to seek to persuade non-Jews. It was Paul, a Greek-speaking Jew and a Roman citizen, who 20 to 30 years after the crucifixion set out to convert the pagans when he failed to win over the Jews resident outside Palestine. It is Paul who must be recognized today as the real founder of Christianity. He fought with Jewish Christians and obtained the other apostles' agreement to exempt his pagan flock from the obligation to adopt Judaism and undergo circumcision in order to become Christians. But Jesus' message, which was directed towards Jews alone, was centred on the Law of Moses which he aimed to renew internally by insisting on its spiritual significance.

Do we know why Jesus died?

Jesus was arrested on the eve of Passover by the Jewish authorities, and was subsequently delivered to the Romans and was crucified. This horrible death on the cross lies at the heart of Christianity.

The only event that can explain his arrest by the Jewish authorities of Jerusalem is the upheaval he caused when he attacked the merchants in the Temple. This happened in the midst of the preparations for Passover with a surcharged atmosphere of the city which was under Roman occupation. Although he was not a political rebel, he incited trouble during a revolutionary period. The provocative attitude he displayed before the priestly authorities – 'I will answer you if you tell me what you think of John the Baptist' – did not help the situation.

How can the resurrection be explained?

For the evangelists, and afterwards for the Church, the proof of the resurrection consisted in the numerous apparitions after the death of Jesus. One can also think that the apostles, traumatized by the cross, needed to feel that Jesus was with them and experience again his charisma for carrying on with their mission and announcing their message. According to the Acts of the Apostles, reinforced by the Holy Spirit, they continued to heal in the name of Jesus who was believed to support them having risen in their hearts.

Did Jesus think that he was of divine nature?

The texts must be read in their context.

The phrase 'son of God' was current among Jews and was synonymous with 'son of Israel' or 'a Jew very close to God'. Jesus' deification was progressive. The first Jesus, the Jesus of the Synoptics, was a healer and a teacher. In the Acts of the Apostles he was a prophet, Lord and Messiah. In Paul, he became 'Son of

God' after the resurrection, and a universal redeemer. Finally, the Gospel of John written between 100 and 110 CE, the theologically most developed book of the New Testament, turned him into a supernatural being, the eternal Word of God, a stranger from heaven who became human for a short while to reveal the heavenly Father to humankind. It is on this notion, developed by the neo-Platonic philosophy of the Greek Church fathers, that the Christian Creed was built.

5

When You Strip Away All the Pious Fiction, What Is Left of the Real Jesus?

What does Christmas signify today if we discard the festive eating, drinking and merrymaking, inherited from the pagan Yule? Is it a reawakening of childhood imagery, dreaming of, but rarely experiencing, a white snowy morning, with Jesus lying in the manger, greeted by bearded shepherds and three colourful oriental stargazing kings, while in the background angelic choirs sing glory to God? Alas, all this is largely pious fiction.

No one knows the exact date of the birth of Jesus Christ. December 25 was selected by the Western Church only in the 4th century to rival the pre-Christian Roman feast of the Victorious Sun. Nor was Christ born in Year 1 as the era bearing his name continues to pretend. The New Testament locates the event shortly before the death of King Herod which occurred in 4BCE. A 6th-century Roman monk, Dionysius the Small, is guilty of the miscalculation: he wrongly placed the birth of Jesus in the year 753 *ab urbe condita* – after the foundation of the city of Rome – instead of 747 or 748.

So who was this Jewish boy, whose wrongly dated birthday is still commemorated the world over on December 25 (the Orthodox Church celebrations are in early January)? The four evangelists, our chief informants, convey two pictures of Jesus. For John, writing probably shortly after 100 CE, he was the eternal Word of God who became flesh for a brief period before ascending to heaven. The other three Gospels, which predate John by one to three decades, depict Jesus in less elevated terms. Their hero was born circa 6 to 5BCE, and was crucified under Pontius Pilate, Roman governor of Judaea between 26 and 36 CE. They report that Jesus lived with his parents, Joseph and Mary, his four brothers and several sisters in Nazareth in the Galilee ruled by Antipas, Herod's son, and was a carpenter or builder.

The essence of the Jesus story is recorded in Mark, the earliest of the Gospels. It immediately starts with his public career with no reference to his birth, childhood or education. Nor are we told whether Jesus was married. Celibate life was unusual among Jews of his age except among the monkish Essenes, described by first-century CE Jewish writers and the Dead Sea Scrolls. But the Gospels ascribe no Essene connection to Jesus; indeed they represent his religious outlook as flatly contradicting Essenism. His choice of the unmarried state must have sprung from his awareness of a prophetic vocation, which imposed on him renunciation of worldly pleasures in order to keep him constantly alert to divine revelations.

Jesus emerged from obscurity in 29 CE, when he answered John the Baptist's appeal to repentance. When John was arrested by Herod Antipas a little later, Jesus set out to announce the imminent coming of the kingdom of heaven. He preached in Galilean village synagogues, practised charismatic healing and exorcism and became famous as 'the prophet Jesus from Nazareth'. He attracted to himself 12 apostles, mostly local fishermen, and spent his itinerant ministry in the Galilean countryside. He visited villages, vineyards, and fields where lilies grew, but shunned the cities. The Synoptic Gospels record only a single fateful visit to Jerusalem.

He addressed his message to 'the house of Israel' alone and expressly forbade His disciples to approach non-Jews, although occasionally he showed compassion to Gentiles and healed the servant of a Roman centurion from Capernaum and the daughter of a Greek woman from southern Lebanon.

As a teacher, he laid special emphasis on the inner significance and permanent validity of the Law of Moses and revealed his spiritual authority, not by interpreting the Bible, but by curing the sick and delivering the possessed. Like his contemporaries, Jesus attributed illness and sin to the influence of evil spirits and considered healing, exorcism and forgiveness of sins as synonyms. People brought the sick to him after the synagogue service on the Sabbath. Some petty-minded bigots muttered that Jesus was breaching the law of sabbatical rest, but his healing by word or touch did not constitute 'work'.

The non-Christian Jewish historian Flavius Josephus, writing shortly before 100 CE, calls Jesus a 'performer of astonishing deeds'. In Christian terminology, the author of the Acts of the Apostles says the same when talking of 'a man attested by God with mighty works and wonders'.

Jesus distinguished himself from other Jewish charismatics of his time by the added beauty and power of his teaching. He preferred poetic imagery to philosophical ideas. He compared the Kingdom of God to a rich harvest, to a tiny mustard seed mysteriously growing into a tall shrub, and to the leaven that mysteriously turns flour into bread. His parables depict the theocentric world to which Jesus' charismatic activity showed the way. Echoing the prophet Isaiah, he declared that his restoring sight to the blind, hearing to the deaf and life to the dead proved that the reign of God had already begun.

For his repentant followers Jesus prescribed complete trust in God, childlike simplicity and a willingness to surrender themselves and their possessions for the sake of heaven. For him the present exceeded the future in importance. Forward planning was meaningless as the time of this world was fast running out.

The ingredients of Jesus' religion were enthusiasm, urgency, compassion and love. He cherished children, the sick and the despised. In his eyes, the return of a stray lamb to the sheepfold, the repentance of a tax-collector or a harlot, caused more joy in heaven than the prosaic virtue of 99 just men.

Because of his healings, many saw in Jesus the Messiah, triumphant over Rome and establisher of everlasting peace. Yet he had no political ambition. Rumours that he might be the Christ were nevertheless spreading and contributed to his downfall. His tragic end was precipitated by an unpremeditated act in the Temple. The noisy business transacted by the merchants of sacrificial animals and the moneychangers so outraged the rural holy man that he overturned their tables and violently expelled them. He thus created a fracas in the sanctuary of the overcrowded city before Passover and alerted the priests.

So the Temple authorities, the official guardians of peace, saw in Jesus a potential threat to order. They had to intervene promptly. Nevertheless even in those circumstances, the Jewish leadership preferred to pass the ultimate responsibility to the cruel Roman governor, Pontius Pilate, who condemned Jesus to death. He was crucified before Passover probably in 30 CE because in the eyes of officialdom, Roman and Jewish, he had done the wrong thing in the wrong place at the wrong time.

Just as the New Testament had prefaced the biography of Jesus by the joyful prologue of the Nativity, it also appended an epilogue to the tragedy of the Cross, the glorious hymn of the Resurrection. Indeed, Jesus had made such a profound impact on his apostles that they attributed to the power of his name the continued success of their charismatic activity. So Jesus rose from the dead in the hearts of his disciples and he lives on as long as the Christian Church endures.

6

Jesus Was a Great Man

The glaring headline 'Jesus was not the Son of God' revealed the intellectual metamorphosis of the much respected Richard Holloway, retired bishop of the Scottish Episcopal Church. Jesus was neither 'literally nor biologically' divine, he claimed, but simply 'an extraordinary man'. No doubt, this episcopal proclamation will create a paroxysm of rage not only among traditional believers, but even among Christmas churchgoers who cherish rosy ideas learnt at Sunday school.

So who was Jesus? Did he exist? Was he God? Is he still relevant? To start with, the existence of Jesus is no longer debatable. He was crucified under Pontius Pilate, Roman governor of Judaea between 26 and 36 CE, and was most probably born shortly before the death of Herod the Great in 4 BCE. Quasi-certainty stops here. To the questions what sort of man Jesus was, what he stood for, what he thought of God and man, what he aimed at achieving during his short career, there are no definite answers.

The primary culprit is Jesus himself. Everything would be different if he had put on paper (better, on leather or papyrus) his thoughts. But, as he wrote nothing, we have to rely on secondary evidence.

Our principal source for Jesus is the New Testament, a collection of writings dating from 25 to 90 years after Christ's death. None of these works is strictly historical, but we can squeeze more information from approximately contemporaneous Jewish documents.

As bad luck would have it, the earliest documents, the letters of St Paul, are of no assistance for the reconstruction of the life of Jesus. Paul never met him. His knowledge mostly depends on his mystical vision, revealing Christ as the universal Saviour of humanity.

Our second bad luck concerns the Gospel of John, a portrait of Jesus as a 'stranger from heaven', composed in the early second century, and reflecting no historical reality.

So we are left with the Gospels of Mark, Matthew and Luke. They are not perfect sources as they have been retouched by a doctrinal brush. Nevertheless they have the form of (popular) biographies of Jesus. The oldest, Mark, concerned only with the public career of Jesus, has no nativity or visions of the risen Christ.

The three reveal Jesus as an itinerant Galilean charismatic healer and preacher. He was not the first, nor the last in this line of holy men. Healing in the ancient Jewish world often took the form of exorcism because sickness, the sequel of sin, had the devil as its cause. So healing the sick and forgiving sins were interchangeable notions. Jesus' practice resembled faith-healing performed in all ages.

The evangelists tell us Jesus was loved by simple people, but scandalized the small-minded village lawyers. He was also resented by his jealous neighbours in Nazareth and his relations thought he was crazy.

His admirers venerated him as a prophet and his name was linked, without his prompting, to that of the Messiah. His preaching showed him as the man entrusted by God to lead his Jewish contemporaries through the gate of repentance into the spiritual promised land. The Messiah was known also as a 'Son of God', the title of the Jewish king in biblical times, but it was never taken by Jews in the literal sense.

The claim that Jesus was also a political Messiah is unfounded. If he had been condemned as an enemy of the state, his followers, too, would have been attacked by the Romans, but they were not.

Why then was Jesus executed? Because he did the wrong thing in the wrong place at the wrong time. The wrong thing was the affray he created in the merchants' quarter in the Temple. The wrong place was the Temple itself where enormous crowds assembled, forming a potential hotbed of revolution. The wrong time was the week before Passover, when multitudes of pilgrims turned Jerusalem into chaos at the Feast of Liberation. Arrested by nervous Temple authorities as a threat to peace, Jesus was handed over to Pilate, whose legionaries crucified him. Pilate was notoriously cruel.

So how can the 'real' Jesus be summed up? He was not meek and mild. He could be impatient and angry. He displayed the strength, iron character and fearlessness of his prophetic predecessors. He loved children, welcomed women, and felt pity for the sick and miserable. He sought the company of the pariahs of Jewish society.

He was convinced of the instant arrival of God's kingdom. So even if he had intended to start a new religion, which he did not, there was no time for the establishment of a church. He acted as a reformer within Judaism. Christianity resulted from St Paul's triumphant preaching of the Gospel in the Graeco-Roman world.

To echo Bishop Holloway, Jesus was an 'extraordinary man', wholly God-centred, passionately faith-inspired and under the imperative impulse of the here and now. He taught men how to appreciate the present moment. He made such an impression on his disciples that not even the cross could cancel his continued real presence. This presence compelled them to carry on in his name their mission and they saw in their success the proof that Jesus was alive in and through them. Here, as someone remarked, lies the real Easter miracle.

How does the face of this 'real' Jesus affect people today? Convinced Christians may be determined to close their eyes and continue in the footsteps of their fathers. Yet even they can learn some worldly wisdom in religion straight from the mouth of the holy man from Galilee.

But the appeal of this Jesus is perhaps strongest for those who are not, are no longer, or have never been, part of the Christian fold, the 'lost sheep' of mankind. They are likely to discover that what Jesus taught about trust in God and compassion for man outweighs all the Christological speculations accumulated over centuries.

7

Benedict XVI and Jesus of Nazareth: A Review

I learnt about the imminent appearance of Pope Benedict XVI's book on Jesus at the University of Princeton in May 2007. I attended there an international conference on methodology in the quest for the historical Jesus where I was to give the opening address. The title, *Jesus of Nazareth*,[1] not 'Jesus, the Son of God' or something similar, seemed to imply that the Pope was one of us, a seeker after historical truth. Indeed, his preface explicitly states that his study incorporates modern historical criticism, and is intended to portray Jesus as a 'historical' figure 'in the strict sense of the word'. I must confess, however, that my initial reaction was over optimistic.

For the benefit of readers not fully conversant with modern Jesus research, blind faith in the literal truth of the Gospels ended, and enlightenment began, in the late 1700s. For more than a century, the German liberal Protestant practitioners of the 'quest for the historical Jesus' engaged in the analysis of the Gospels qua ancient religious texts. Their search produced two diametrically opposite portraits: Jesus, the liberal teacher of exalted Jewish morality, and Jesus, the herald of the imminent catastrophic onset of a new world, the Kingdom of God. The two theories turned out to be irreconcilable, and in 1906 Albert Schweitzer concluded the first quest, and declared the historical Jesus dead.

After the First World War, Gospel research restarted under the inspiration of the German form-critical school, founded by Rudolf Bultmann. He believed that the study of 'the life and personality of Jesus' was doomed because the earliest Christian sources were interested only in the faith of the Church. Instead, the task of the scholar was to distinguish various literary forms (proverbs, parables, controversies, apocalyptic prophecies) in the transmitted material and to locate them in early church history and, occasionally, in the story of Jesus. Hence, 1920 to 1950 was the period of 'no quest'.

However, despite Schweitzer's funeral oration, the historical Jesus refused to lie down. Around 1950, a new attempt to retrieve him was launched in Germany by Bultmann's pupils, who reemployed the form-critical method in the pursuit of historical research. The 'new' or 'second quest' went on for some 20 years without much success. It coincided with the years of Joseph Ratzinger's theological studies. However, he did not specialize as a *Neutestamentler*, but as a patristic scholar and dogmatic theologian.

The 1970s and 1980s introduced the 'third quest'. By then, the dominance of German professors, with Hellenistic expertise to deal with Greek Gospels but without direct familiarity with the Jewish world of the age of Jesus, came to an end. They were replaced by British and American scholars concerned with the discovery, partly associated with the Dead Sea Scrolls, of the 'Jewish' Jesus. The literary landmarks of the new era were *Jesus the Jew*[2] (1973) by your reviewer and *Jesus and Judaism*[3] (1986) by E. P. Sanders, both professors at Oxford. In no time, the search for the Jewish Jesus became dominant worldwide. By then, Roman Catholic scholars, too, came to the fore, having been debarred until the 1940s from participating in critical Bible research by the Vatican's Pontifical Biblical Commission.

The change came about so promptly because academics and educated lay people realized that, in order to encounter the Jesus of flesh and blood, one had to break through the barrier constituted by the translation into Greek of the original Semitic, Aramaic-Hebrew, cultural and religious traditions aimed at the non-Jewish Christians of Syria, Asia Minor, Egypt, Greece and Italy. Remember the saying, every translator is a traitor.

Turning to the Pope's book, its ten chapters cover the career of Jesus from his baptism to Peter's confession and the Transfiguration, with full chapters assigned to the gospel of the Kingdom, the sermon on the mount, the Lord's prayer, the parables, images in

John's Gospel and a few titles of Jesus. It is a haphazard mixture of life and doctrine.

In his preface, the scholar Ratzinger bravely declares that he and not the Pope is the author of the book and that everyone is free to contradict him. I was first tempted to say, 'Yes, I will', but quickly realized that a frontal assault on *Jesus of Nazareth* from the standpoint of present-day Gospel criticism would be inappropriate. The Pope was engaged not in academic research but in a series of meditations on the Gospels for his own and his readers' edification. The efficacy of these meditations cannot be judged by academic criteria.

Nevertheless, we are told that the Pope obeyed the rules of historical criticism. However, he was prepared to abide by those rules only if they confirmed his traditional convictions. Otherwise, he discarded them without further consideration. As he refuses to examine various possibilities of meaning, he must take it for granted that he has the correct understanding. But how can this be if no critical questions are asked about the original significance of words?

For a scholarly critic, one of the most disturbing aspects of the book is the absence of reference to texts that in some way contradict Benedict's cherished beliefs. For instance, he finds in the Gospels scores of allusions to the divinity of Christ. They are all made explicit by the Pope and considered as proven. Yet, try as you may, nowhere will you read in this 'Gospel according to Benedict' that Jesus refused to accept the title 'Good Master' on the grounds that it would implicitly suggest that he possessed a divine quality. 'Why do you call me good? No one is good but God alone' (Mark 10.18). Another recurrent theme in Ratzinger's perception of Christ is that Jesus intended the Gospel to be preached to all the nations. If so, did he just forget Jesus' sayings that contradict the universality of the apostolic mission, namely, that both Jesus and his disciples were sent only to the 'lost sheep of Israel' (Matt. 10.5–6; 15.24).

Be all this as it may, in fairness, one must concede that the Pope is free to find his spiritual solace wherever he chances upon it, and to communicate his insights to all those willing to share them.

Yet I must protest against the reiterated papal claim that the divine Christ of faith – the product of his musings – and the historical Jesus – the Galilean itinerant healer, exorcist and preacher – are one and the same. In the absence of a stringent linguistic, literary and historical analysis of the Gospels, especially of their many contradictory statements, the identification is without foundation. One must declare groundless Benedict's appeal to 'canonical exegesis', an exercise in biblical theology whereby any text from the Old or the New Testament can serve to explain any other biblical text. Such an approach to biblical studies would force back Catholic Bible experts, already the objects of frequent papal disapproval in *Jesus of Nazareth*, to a pre-Copernican stage of history.

As a final comment, may I, after a lifetime of study of Judaism and early Christianity and in the light of hundreds of letters inspired by my books, voice the conviction that the powerful, inspirational and, above all, real figure of the historical Jesus is able to exercise a profound influence on our age, especially on people who are no longer impressed by traditional Christianity. While scholarly exegesis removes some of the mystery enveloping the Church's Christ, it does not throw out the baby with the bathwater. Contrary to Pope Benedict's forebodings, the world would welcome this authentic Jesus.

Notes

1 Pope Benedict XVI, 2007, *Jesus of Nazareth: From the Baptism in the Jordan to the Transfiguration*, London: Bloomsbury.

2 Geza Vermes, 1973, *Jesus the Jew*, London: SCM Press.

3 E. P. Sanders, 1986, *Jesus and Judaism*, London: SCM Press.

8

The Truth about the Historical Jesus

There are two kinds of truth about Jesus Christ. The first is the Gospel truth. Its veracity is vouchsafed by faith. In the believer's eyes no contradictions do, or even can, exist in the divinely inspired Gospels. Appearances to the contrary should be ignored or reconciled.

For instance, the Gospel of John gives a historically acceptable account of the condemnation of Jesus: he was arrested a day before Passover and, without the mention of a Passover meal and a formal Jewish court process, he was brought before Pilate, accused of being a revolutionary and sentenced to crucifixion.

In the other Gospels, in a historically unlikely fashion, the arrest of Jesus, followed by a trial by the Jewish Sanhedrin on the charge of blasphemy, took place after the Passover meal (the Last Supper), and Jesus was pronounced guilty on the night of the feast itself. Yet no believing Christian asks how the supreme tribunal of Judaea could try a capital case during one of the major festivals – or, more simply, how the two stories hang together.

The second kind of truth is less certain than faith and is approximated by means of 'scientific' historical inquiry. This quest strives to discover the *truth*, but succeeds in retrieving only morsels of it. The historian's task is to assemble a monumental jigsaw puzzle of which many parts are still missing. My catchy title for this article promises more than anyone can deliver. A more modest 'Towards the truth about the historical Jesus' would be closer to what will follow.

Until the mid-eighteenth century, gospel truth wholly dominated the Christian world and it has continued to do so in conservative ecclesiastical circles up to the present day. This certainty did not result from the blinding effect that faith exerted on the historical evidence. As early as the second century, divergences among the New Testament records were noted by perspicacious Church fathers and a deliberate attempt was made to harmonize them, producing the so-called *Diatessaron*, the four Gospels in one. But after some initial success the innovation failed and the traditional four Gospels survived.

Thus later Church fathers were perfectly aware that the two genealogies of Jesus in Matthew and in Luke were incompatible, but they launched the seemingly brilliant idea that Matthew traced the ancestry of Jesus through Joseph, while Luke did so through Mary. They turned a blind eye to the fact that among Jews a genealogy was expected to follow the male line.

The quest for the human figure of Jesus began with Samuel Reimarus in the mid-eighteenth century and has characterized academic Gospel criticism up to the present day. For the first 200 years it was essentially a German academic pursuit, although from the late nineteenth century onwards there was a smattering of British, French and American contributions. It aimed at the rediscovery of the 'historical Jesus' and sought to distinguish him from the 'Christ of faith'. Its initial stage ended with the anticlimactic *Geschichte der Leben Jesu Forschung* (Quest of the Historical Jesus) by Albert Schweitzer,[1] who in 1906 described the whole process as far too subjective to be worthy of continuation. According to Schweitzer, each scholar produced a Jesus in his own image and resemblance.

From the 1920s to the 1950s, research into the historical Jesus became rather unfashionable under the influence of Rudolf Bultmann, the great German scholar, and his new literary–critical school of *Formgeschichte* or form criticism. In 1926, he advanced the memorable statement that in effect excommunicated Life of Jesus inquiry in the wide academic circles over which he ruled: 'We can know almost nothing about the life and personality of Jesus since the early Christian sources show no interest in either.' For Bultmann, the setting of the gospel message was not the life of Jesus; the evangelists were catering for the needs of the nascent Church. After a 30-year silence the historical interest was slowly rekindled in Germany; it was short-lived and without noteworthy results.

In the 1970s, for the first time in two centuries, the main scene of activity left Germany. It first moved to England, and soon after to the United States. The principal emphasis lay not on the Hellenistic background of the early Church as in form criticism but on the Jewishness of Jesus in the wake of the discovery of the Dead Sea Scrolls and the renewal of research into post-biblical Judaism and Flavius Josephus, the Jewish historian of the first century CE.

The trend is clearly shown by the new titles: *Jesus the Jew* (1973),[2] *Jesus and Judaism* (1985),[3] *The Historical Jesus: The Life of a Mediterranean Jewish Peasant* (1991);[4] *A Marginal Jew: Rethinking the Historical Jesus* (1991–2001)[5] and *Jesus of Nazareth, King of the Jews: A Jewish Life and the Emergence of Christianity* (1999).[6]

Indeed, during the past quarter of a century, in one way or another, the Jewish Jesus has become the dominant figure in New Testament scholarship, pursued by all researchers with or without religious belief. For the numerous Roman Catholic practitioners of the quest, the whole issue was put back in the melting pot in 2007 by Joseph Ratzinger, i.e. His Holiness Pope Benedict XVI. In a best-selling book, *Jesus of Nazareth*,[7] he declared that the Gospels' Christ of faith *is* the historical Jesus, thus turning the clock back by several centuries. Pope Benedict bravely invites fellow scholars to contradict him if they feel so inclined, but the big question is whether Catholic biblical exegetes will have the courage to join Ratzinger's independent critics.

Now let's face the main issue. The student investigating the problem of the historical Jesus is confronted with a concatenation of difficulties.

Everyone except the desperately naive knows that the Gospel sources are not strictly historical and postdate the events by decades. The earlier letters of St Paul won't help as their author never knew, or showed interest in, the Jesus of flesh and blood. The four Gospels, written between some 15 to 55 years after Paul, in the form of biographies, formulate Jesus' teaching adapted for the needs of the early church.

Moreover, their readers had a Greek linguistic background and a Graeco-Roman cultural background, yet they were to receive a Jewish religious message originally formulated in Aramaic. We are facing the *traduttore traditore* syndrome.

The historical Jesus can be retrieved only within the context of first-century Galilean Judaism. The Gospel image must therefore be inserted into the historical canvas of Palestine in the first century CE, with the help of the works of Flavius Josephus, the Dead Sea Scrolls and early rabbinic literature.

Against this background, what kind of picture of Jesus emerges from the Gospels? That of a rural holy man, initially a follower of the movement of repentance launched by another holy man, John the Baptist. In the hamlets and villages of Lower Galilee and the lakeside, Jesus set out to preach the coming of the Kingdom of God within the lifetime of his generation and outlined the religious duties his simple listeners were to perform to prepare themselves for the great event.

An eloquent popular preacher, Jesus manifested his spiritual power by exorcisms and healing. His audience remarked that 'he taught with authority' – namely, curing the sick and liberating the possessed – and 'not as the scribes', who could only quote the Bible to prove their sayings. His cures consisted in faith-healing: they required trust on the part of the sick. He invited them to believe in his healing power as a man of God. Indeed, he went so far as to identify this faith as the cause of the recovery: 'Your faith has made you well', he reassured a sick woman (Mark 5.4).

In behaving as he did, Jesus conformed to a pattern of charismatic behaviour attested among Jews throughout the ages and down to his own time. The biblical prophets Elisha, Elijah and Isaiah are credited with miraculous healings and resuscitations. Similar phenomena are ascribed in rabbinic literature to holy men living in the age close to the New Testament.

Honi in the first century BCE and the Galilean Hanina ben Dosa in the first century CE were renowned for their miraculous rain-making power; Hanina's fame also comprised healing, including healing from a distance like Jesus, and general wonderworking. Flavius Josephus (37–c.100 CE) reports not only on thaumaturgists of Old Testament vintage, such as Elisha, but explicitly mentions Honi, whose wondrous intervention ended a disastrous drought shortly before Pompey's capture of Jerusalem in 63 BCE. He also refers to Jesus in the days of Pontius Pilate and calls him a 'wise man and performer of astonishing or paradoxical deeds'.

The reliability of Josephus's notice about Jesus was rejected by many in the nineteenth and early twentieth centuries, but it has been judged partly genuine and partly falsified by the majority of more recent critics. The Jesus portrait of Josephus, drawn by an uninvolved witness, stands halfway between the fully sympathetic picture of early Christianity and the wholly antipathetic image of the magician of Talmudic and post-Talmudic Jewish literature. 'Wise man' and 'performer of paradoxical deeds' are genuinely Josephan phrases that no Christian interpolator would have found potent enough to describe the divinized Christ of the later Church.

The contour of the historical Jesus, lifted from the Synoptic Gospels, suggests a magnetic prophetic figure who was convinced that the aim of his mission was to bring his repentant Jewish followers into God's new realm. This kingdom of heaven was foreseen in many of Jesus' parables as the outcome of a quiet and imperceptible change rather than a cataclysmic transformation in the not too distant future. It would seem, according to the evangelists, that Jesus considered himself, and his well-disposed contemporaries depicted him, along such prophetic-charismatic lines.

For example, Jesus explains his rejection by his family and fellow citizens of Nazareth by the well-known saying that at home no one is recognized as a prophet. He was also regularly alluded to by non-local contemporaries as the great prophet from Nazareth. In the anecdote of Caesarea Philippi, Peter's answer to Jesus' question, 'Who do men say that I am?', follows a similar turn. Jesus, Peter said, was believed to be a prophet, or the returning Elijah or John the Baptist revived.

But when pressed to reveal what the circle of disciples thought of Jesus, Peter confessed, according to Mark, that he was the

Messiah, or, according to Matthew, the Messiah with the added synonym of 'the Son of the living God'. The latter phrase was understood in Gentile-Christian theology as a move towards the recognition of the divine status of Jesus.

In the course of my research that led to the writing of *Jesus the Jew*, it was impossible not to notice that Church tradition tended to attribute the maximum of significance to the honorific titles applied to Jesus by the evangelists. I decided therefore to set up a quasi-scientific experiment. I said to myself: let's try to establish the correlation between the features of the Jesus portrait of the Gospels and the meaning of the designations such as 'Messiah', 'Lord' and 'Son of God' in the mind of the contemporaries of Jesus.

To achieve this, we must forget the Greek understanding of the terms by the Gentile readers of the Gospel; get rid of 2,000 years of superimposed Christian interpretation of the New Testament, and switch instead the searchlight on Jesus' Aramaic-speaking Jewish audience on the shore of the Lake of Galilee. What was the original meaning of the message and what did the original addressees make of it?

To start with 'the Messiah', the Greek *Christos*, if a pollster had interrogated the men in the street in Palestine two millennia ago, asking for a definition of 'Messiah', he would have heard people mumbling about the greatest Jewish king, who would defeat the Romans. The more religiously minded would have added that the Messiah would also be just and holy, and would subject all the nations to Israel and to God. In more peripheral circles, such as the Dead Sea sect, several Messiahs were expected, one royal, one priestly and possibly one prophetic.

But even the 'don't-knows' would have had an idea about the messianic age, filled chock-a-block with miraculous events. According to the words put into the mouth of Jesus, this would be the time when 'The blind receive their sight, and the lame walk, lepers are cleansed and the deaf hear' (Matt. 11.5).

Did Jesus present himself or did the evangelists portray him as a warlike royal pretender? The answer must be no. Jesus always forbade his disciples to proclaim him the Messiah, and when confronted with the question 'Are you the Christ?', his regular reply was evasively negative: 'That's what you call me', he kept on saying, 'not I'.

By contrast, the non-bellicose wonderworking figure standing in the shadow of the messianic age fits him perfectly. It tallies with the picture of the Galilean healer, exorcist and preacher so prominent in the Gospels of Mark, Matthew and Luke. In his answer to the question of John the Baptist whether he was the one who was to come, Jesus simply pointed to the events surrounding him: the blind see, the deaf hear, the lame walk, the lepers are healed (Matt. 11; Luke 7.22).

The title 'Lord', *Kyrios* in Greek, carried high associations at this time. It pointed to the emperor, the Lord Caesar, whose Latin epithet was 'divine', as in *divus Augustus*. In turn, among Greek-speaking Jews, whose Bible the early church appropriated, *Kyrios* (Lord) was the regular substitute for the Hebrew four-lettered sacred and secret name of God. Quite naturally, in the Gospel read in the Greek churches, 'the Lord Christ' (*Kyrios Christos*) promptly acquired divine flavour. By contrast, in Jewish circles, with an infinite gap between the divine and the human reality, such a combination was well-nigh inconceivable.

Beside Caesar and God, what other meanings did the title 'Lord' possess? What did the Galileans imply when they addressed Jesus as 'Lord', or *Mar* in Aramaic? The title, reminiscent of 'Sir' in English, could refer to a variety of persons: to a secular dignitary, to the head of the family, to an authoritative teacher, to a prophet and to a miracle-worker. The last three nuances perfectly suit the Jesus portrait of the Synoptic Gospels.

Finally, the appellation 'Son of God', the title in the Hellenistic world of the deified Roman emperor and synonymous with God in early Christianity, is nowhere attested in that sense in Judaism. It is, however, capable of carrying at least five other meanings. It can designate an angel in the superhuman world. In the terrestrial domain, each Jew was entitled to call himself 'son of God'. But the term underwent a series of restrictive interpretations. In the post-exilic age only the Jews whose heart was circumcised and filled with Holy Spirit were allotted that name. Also, both the Bible and the Dead Sea Scrolls assign filial status to the Messiah, metaphorically the son of the living God. Moreover, some charismatic contemporaries of Jesus were referred to as sons of God. For example, Honi, who managed to produce rain by pestering God, was compared to a son importuning his long-suffering and loving father.

Finally, there is the image of the divine voice from heaven proclaiming someone the 'son of God'. This is reported about the Galilean Hanina ben Dosa. Both sayings indicate that in Jewish parlance 'son of God' implies divine favour rather than the sharing of the divine nature.

To recapitulate, the philological, literary and historical analysis of the Semitic meaning of Jesus' titles corroborates his image as it emerges from the Synoptic Gospels. Hence the only reasonable conclusion to draw from a combined study of the Gospel picture and the honorific titles is that the historical Jesus was a Galilean charismatic whose aim was to conduct his repentant Palestinian Jewish contemporaries into the spiritual realm called the Kingdom of God through preaching, healing and exorcizing.

Traditional Christianity does not stop at this portrait of the human Jesus, but overlays it with the majestic image of the Christ of faith arising from the mystical meditations of Paul and John and the Hellenistic philosophy of the Greek Church Fathers.

In a nutshell, Jesus' preaching was centred on God, the heavenly Father, on the dignity of all human beings as children of God, on life turned into worship by total trust, on an overwhelming sense of urgency to do one's duty without procrastination, on the sanctification of the here and now, and above all on the love of God through the love of one's neighbour.

To conclude, because of the cross, the task of Jesus remained unfinished. Yet despite the apparent failure of his mission, his magnetic impact was so profound that, instead of abandoning the cause, his disciples began to look forward to his imminent second coming. When by the mid-second century Jesus failed to return, Jewish Christianity progressively faded away, while St Paul's Gentile church survived and after Constantine set out to flourish – albeit in a form that I believe would have perplexed Jesus the Jew.

Notes

1 Albert Schweitzer, 2000, *The Quest for the Historical Jesus* (new ed.), London: SCM Press.

2 Geza Vermes, 1973, *Jesus the Jew*, London: SCM Press.

3 Geza Vermes, 1983, *Jesus and Judaism*, London: SCM Press.

4 John Dominic Crossan, 1992, *The Historical Jesus: The Life of a Mediterranean Jewish Peasant*, HarperCollins.

5 John P. Meier, 1991, *A Marginal Jew: Rethinking the Historical Jesus*, London: Continuum.

6 Paula Fredriksen, 1999, *Jesus of Nazareth, King of the Jews: A Jewish Life and the Emergence of Christianity*, New York: Knopf.

7 Pope Benedict XVI, 2007, *Jesus of Nazareth: From the Baptism in the Jordan to the Transfiguration*, London: Bloomsbury.

9

Was Jesus Really Human?

Christology, the Christian doctrine about Jesus, can be summed up in one sentence slightly paraphrasing the poetic prologue of the Fourth Gospel: 'The eternal Word of God became flesh to dwell among us' (John 1.14). For the Church, the little babe, produced by Mary in the dying days of King Herod the Great, was simultaneously and truly human and divine.

Faith can cope with such an apparent self-contradiction on the grounds that for God everything is possible. So the baffled Virgin was indeed reassured by the angel of the Annunciation, when she wondered about the possibility of conceiving a child without 'knowing' a man. Early Christians, many of them nurtured from childhood by classical culture, found this enigma profoundly disturbing. As a result, controversies started to rage almost at once in the Church about the relation of Jesus to God. From 100 CE to the fifth century, patriarchs, bishops and theologians, steeped in Hellenistic philosophy, tried to impose on their opponents their favourite solution to the dilemma amid vehement debates in ecumenical councils, convened in ancient Greek cities situated in Asiatic Turkey: Nicaea, Ephesus, Chalcedon.

Confronted with the question of Jesus' duality – was he God or was he man? – thinking people of today would find the second alternative the safer option. However, even a cursory glance at ancient Church history reveals that in early Christianity the opposite tendency often prevailed. Religious thinkers in the early centuries of the present era had no difficulty in accepting Jesus' divinity. What they questioned from late New Testament times onwards (1 John 4.2) was the reality of his flesh. They belonged to the school of thought called 'docetism' or the theory of appearance.

According to their logic while truly divine, Christ was not really human and consequently being God, he could not die. Some docetists indeed suggested that it was not Jesus, but Judas Iscariot or Simon of Cyrene who was vicariously crucified on behalf of Christ, the immortal God. Islam, too, inherited the same idea.

The first major Christian attempt to square the Christological circle was made at the Council of Nicaea in 325 CE, on account of the teaching of Arius, an Egyptian theologian, who asserted that Christ was not of the same substance as God the Father: he was not an eternal being. 'There was a time when the Word (*Logos*) did not exist', was the slogan of the Arians parading in the streets of Alexandria in the early fourth century. In response, the Fathers of the Council of Nicaea, presided over by the first Christian Emperor Constantine, decreed that Christ was God, being of the same divine essence or substance (*ousia*) as the Father. He was consubstantial (*homoousios*) with him. The manhood of Jesus remained untouched in Nicaea. The Fathers of the Council held the shadowy belief that in the person of the incarnate Christ humanity and divinity mysteriously co-existed.

The problem of the unity or duality of the person and nature of Jesus continued to haunt the Church after Nicaea. In the first half of the fifth century both questions were addressed. First Nestorius, a Syrian theologian, claimed he had resolved the riddle of the relation between divinity and humanity by advancing the thesis that in the incarnate Christ there were *two persons*, one divine, the other human. But this doctrine carried an unpalatable logical consequence. If in Christ there were two separate persons, Mary could be the mother of only the *man* Jesus, and should henceforth no longer be venerated under the traditional title of 'God-bearer' (*Theotokos*). This was a touchy subject because to the pious fifth-century worshippers anything diminishing the stature of the Virgin sounded scandalous. So in 431 CE the Council of Ephesus condemned the heresy of Nestorius, and recognized in Christ only *one divine person*, thus vindicating the traditional worship of the Mother of God.

After the Council of Ephesus, the Constantinopolitan monk Eutyches, wishing to sharpen his attack on Nestorianism, proclaimed that with the Incarnation the one person of Christ possessed only a single nature (*physis*) which was *divine*. Jesus' manhood was unreal; it was not the same as ours. The Council of Chalcedon in 451 CE anathematized his error, called Monophysitism ('one-nature-ism'), and defined as the Church's faith that in the *single person* of Christ there exist, 'without confusion, without change, without division, without separation', *two natures*, one divine and immortal, the other human and mortal.

In official Church teaching this line of thought – one person, two natures – has remained the orthodox belief until the present day. Yet, in practical terms over the centuries in Christian teaching and preaching Jesus has chiefly been regarded as God. His humanity was needed only for the doctrine of atonement through the death of the Redeemer. But in all other respects, in the theological thinking of the Church his true manhood was completely overshadowed by his divinity. The German Jesuit Karl Rahner, perhaps the greatest dogmatist of the twentieth century, had the courage to point a finger at this *crypto*-Monophysite trend of basic Christian religiosity.[1]

Academic scriptural research, employing the tools of modern critical method in its investigation of the New Testament, offers unwitting support for Chalcedon's 'two nature' doctrine when it distinguishes the human *Jesus of history* from the divine *Christ of faith*. Yet even today conservative Churchmen are frightened from following the path leading to Jesus of Nazareth, the charismatic Jewish prophet of the earliest Gospels. In their eyes – mistakenly I believe – the human Jesus is a threat to the Christ of theological interpretation.

Note

1 Karl Rahner, 1961, 'Current Problems in Christology', in *Theological Investigations* vol. I, London: Darton, Longman & Todd, pp. 149–200.

10

A Television Documentary on Christ and the British Press: Channel 4's *Jesus: the Evidence* (April 1984)

Nowadays TV documentaries on Jesus, mostly of a sensation-seeking kind, are 13 to the dozen. The conventionally pious watch them and hate them. The agnostics and atheists feel duty bound to applaud them. And the uncommitted, that is the large majority of the viewing public, switch on the programmes, quickly get bored and move to another channel. The then still new Channel 4, set up in November 1982, created sensation by scheduling three weekly 60-minute broadcasts by London Weekend Television (LWT). Directed by a prize-winning documentary maker, D. Rolfe, it was given the mysterious and exciting title, *Jesus: the Evidence*. It was meant to subject the traditional image of Jesus to a critical scrutiny and sketch a fresh portrait in the light of the new findings.

My own involvement with the project began in late 1982, when I was consulted by Jean-Claude Braggard, a young researcher who, I was told, had been reading one book a day on the topic for the previous five months. By journalistic standards he showed himself fairly knowledgeable. What is your background, I asked him. He had read PPE (Philosophy, Politics and Economics) in Oxford, he replied. It seemed to provide the master key to any subject.

I learned from him the plan of *Jesus: the Evidence*. The first part of the series would trace the history of New Testament scholarship from the late eighteenth to the mid-twentieth century. The second would depict attitudes current in the 1980s, and the final part would survey the development of Christianity from the empty tomb to the Council of Nicaea where the divinity of Jesus was defined in 325 CE. The participants would be well-known experts: Professors Werner Kümmel, successor of Rudolf Bultmann at Marburg, and Dennis Nineham, former Regius Professor of Divinity in Cambridge and Warden of Keble College Oxford; Canon Anthony Harvey of Westminster Abbey, author of *Jesus and the Constraints of History*,[1] myself, Reader in Jewish Studies in Oxford and author of *Jesus the Jew*;[2] Professors Helmut Koester, a pupil of Bultmann and holder of the chair of the New Testament and Early Church History at Harvard Divinity School and G. Quispel, renowned Dutch Church historian. Three more controversial characters, Professors George Wells, of Birkbeck College, London, Morton Smith of Columbia University, New York, and Ian Wilson of Turin Shroud notoriety would also contribute. As a last minute balancing act, the organizers invited also Professor Howard Marshall of Aberdeen University, entrusted with the defence of conventional Christianity. The team seemed fairly well balanced and I agreed to participate. One might say that on the whole this was a weightier scholarly team than those displayed nowadays in religious documentaries.

What about the end product? The programme was basically satisfactory, though I strongly disapproved of the acting bits, of the phony German accent in English imposed on thespians playing Albert Schweitzer and Rudolf Bultmann. I would have preferred not to have Professor Wells with his half-baked theory of the non-existence of Jesus and the equally unsound innuendoes of Morton Smith concerning male nudity and homosexuality associated with his concept of the revelation of the Kingdom of God. But in fairness to the film makers it should be stressed that the viewers were made aware that neither Wells nor Smith represented mainstream scholarship.

However, this reasoned criticism of mine is poles apart from the hysteria that seized most of the British press, especially the religious weeklies, long before *Jesus: the Evidence* was first shown to the public. Apparently an early draft of the project was leaked to the evangelical journal *Buzz*, whose editor demanded and obtained a preview of parts I and II of the series. All hell broke loose on poor Channel 4. 'Fasten your seatbelts' – ran *Buzz*'s caption – 'for LWT [is going to] to undermine the biblical view of Christ'. On account of Morton Smith's and Ian Wilson's comments, the programme was caricatured as representing Jesus as a master of the occult who practised nocturnal baptisms with homosexual overtones and performed 'miracles' through hypnosis. The editor of *Buzz*, a certain Steve Goddard, also complained that the only 'conservative', that is to say reliable, participant (Professor Marshall) was granted only a miserly 59 seconds to expound 'the truth'. Be all this as it may, *Buzz* gave the clarion call for an anti-*Jesus: the Evidence* crusade.

The week before the screening of the first instalment, the Methodist Church issued an official criticism of the programme. *The Times* (5 April) quoted the Free Church religious adviser of LWT, himself a Methodist clergyman, who claimed that the series was to air the views of 'eccentric scholars'. The next day a working party of Roman Catholic biblical specialists, convoked by Cardinal Basil Hume, spoke of 'glaring weaknesses' that rendered the 'tendentious' programme 'more than suspect'. The harsh denunciation was followed by a quick Catholic backtracking, admitting that 'a large number of scholars, including Catholic scholars, would have no difficulty in accepting that . . . the titles attributed to Jesus in the Gospels (e.g. 'Son of God') were not in fact used during his lifetime'. And again: 'Jesus, as a Jew, is hardly likely to have claimed to be God'. But there was no such caution in the *Catholic Herald* (6 April). A Father Nicholas Murphy SJ called *Jesus: the Evidence* 'a load of drivel', and finished his tirade with a not very Christian proposition: 'The researcher ought to be shot!'

Nevertheless, the tone of the *Catholic Herald* was mild compared with that of the strange bedfellows, *Private Eye* and the *Church Times*. They blamed the outrage on foreigners, on 'outdated German scholarship'. The role of the British contingent was played down or ignored. Nineham was said to appear only 'briefly'; Harvey as English as they can make it (Eton, Oxford, Westminster Abbey) was forgotten and I seem to have been ranked among 'the German or American' participants. The venerable *Church Times* beat them all in silliness. The editor dispatched a certain Betty Saunders to the preview and she wrote a front page article castigating the TV series for casting doubt on the truth of the Gospel. Betty Saunders attacked one of the contributors to the documentary, Rudolf Bultmann! She did not realize that the person appearing on the screen was an actor and not Bultmann who was by then dead and buried for eight years.

We were still before the showing of the first instalment, and the scene of action moved from Fleet Street to the House of Commons, where the Tory MP for Swindon successfully demanded a previewing of *Jesus: the Evidence,* as reported by the *Observer* of 8 April. A letter was sent by him from the palace of Westminster to the controller of Channel 4 requesting the postponement of the programme for six months. Not unexpectedly the demand was turned down and the first episode was duly broadcast on 8 April.

While the free pre-publicity considerably increased the viewing numbers, the TV critics of the London press reacted with patronizing condescension. 'Vaguely vulgar', ran the headline of *The Times.* The *Guardian* spoke of a 'holy mess' and the *Times Educational Supplement* blamed the producer for incompetence as he allowed an actor to play Bultmann without sporting a moustache!

Once the films themselves, and not merely rumours, had to be considered, the dust began to settle. Of course, the *Church Times* continued to stick to its guns and informed its readers that 're-spected scholars and theologians' judged the series 'mischievous, misleading and unbalanced'. *The Church of England Newspaper* (13 April) held me personally responsible for the groundwork on which the film proceeded. It objected to the *'lengthy* assessment of Jesus' I was allowed to formulate, while Canon Harvey provided only 'a brief interlude'. The law of relativity seems to be at work in gauging the length of time allotted to participants. Those with whom the reviewers agree stay far too briefly on the screen; those they dislike remain there for ever. In fact Harvey and I were granted exactly the same air time.

There were solitary voices sympathetic to the programme. The *Sunday Times* (8 April) described it as 'a decent popular statement of the present state of New Testament scholarship'. *The Listener* (12 April) in turn almost overstated the favourable case: 'It was hard to see how anyone but the most fanatical literalist could have been offended by a scrupulously phrased, lucid and quite fascinating script, in which 100 years of biblical scholarship were summarized, leaving one hungry for more.'

Two-thirds through the series, the secular media, with a few exceptions, altogether lost interest in *Jesus: the Evidence*, whereas a semblance of sanity affected the non-Anglican religious papers. The *Catholic Herald* changed its original approach (remember Fr Murphy's 'The researcher ought to be shot') and came up with the revolutionary idea of asking a Scripture expert to reflect on the films. Their reviewer, the Benedictine Fr Henry Wansborough, later Master of St Benet's Hall, Oxford, dared write: 'It is undeniable that Jesus never calls himself God in the Gospels, and it would be a strange revealer who deliberately held back so vital an element in his consciousness . . . Vermes is right: to a Palestinian Jew of this time the idea would indeed have been inconceivable.'

If the *Catholic Herald* adopted a serious tone, the *Methodist Recorder*'s reviewer, Kenneth Grayston, emeritus professor of Theology at Bristol, followed a light-hearted approach (19 April). He qualified the film an 'overstuffed first-year undergraduate lecture', less coherent than those Grayston himself used to give, but 'more lavishly illustrated'. Talking about the academic 'mavericks and eccentrics' of the *Buzz* school of thought, Grayston scored heavily against his rivals. He happened to know all the contributors personally. 'Professor Nineham, my friend and successor, has the gift of asking disturbing questions; Professor Kümmel is a very balanced scholar who was (presumably) paid to say what every student knows . . . Geza Vermes is confident that Josephus, the Jewish historian of those days, referred to Jesus (thus upsetting Professor Wells who thinks Jesus did not exist).' Grayston then concluded: 'I wonder how many people in our congregations know enough about the contents of the Gospels to realise what the fuss is about.'

The fuss was attributed by Gerald Priestland, religious affairs correspondent of the BBC, to the conservatism and theological illiteracy of the clergy. 'Too often the demand for balance turns out to be a demand that the scales should come crushing down on the side of orthodoxy.' On the other hand, Chris Dunkley, the TV critic of the *Financial Times*, was equally firm in placing the blame on the shoulders of the media moguls. 'Up to now TV has been pusillanimous about religion. First the BBC, then the ITV, have become mouthpieces of Christianity. That is to say, TV's function in journalism as a seeker after facts has been virtually ignored so far as religion is concerned. LWT's series was an attempt to investigate the evidence on which the Jesus belief rests and do it in three hours. It is a pity they did not have ten more episodes . . . The hostility shown to *Jesus: the Evidence* reeks of the same intolerant fear of facts that was displayed by the Inquisition when they threatened Galileo with the rack in order to force him to recant his fearful heresy.'

The fuss surrounding *Jesus: the Evidence* was meant to be brought to an end at a round table discussion organized by Channel 4 on 29 April 1984. The good-looking lady theologian Ann Loades of Durham University chaired the chat show whose participants used first names, John, Henry, Hyam, Tom and Howard. They were Canon John Fenton of Christ Church, Oxford, Henry Chadwick, Regius Professor of Divinity successively in both Cambridge and Oxford and for a while Dean of Christ Church, Hyam Maccoby of Leo Baeck College, the Tom in question whose other name I have forgotten was a Jesuit from Heythrop College, London, and the evangelical Howard Marshall was at last allowed to clock up a few extra minutes additional to his original 59 seconds. On the whole, the illustrious team agreed with the mainline message of *Jesus: the Evidence*.

A happy ending of the story? Not quite. On the day when LWT held what the *Church Times* termed its 'inquest on Jesus' the issues raised in the Channel 4 series were also discussed in ITV's religious programme, *Credo*. In the course of the debate, one of the speakers, by the name of David Jenkins, then professor of Theology at Leeds University, but also Bishop-designate of

Durham, made the famous statement on the Nativity: 'I wouldn't put it past God to arrange for a virgin birth if he wanted to, but I very much doubt if he would.' He also called the Resurrection 'a series of experiences' rather than an event. He thus reopened the questions treated in *Jesus: the Evidence*, upset many and, according to some, brought down fire from heaven on York Minster a few weeks later on 9 July 1984.

The modern age in religious TV documentaries began.

Notes

1 A.E Harvey, 1982, *Jesus and the Constraints of History*, London: Duckworth.

2 Geza Vermes, 1973, *Jesus the Jew*, London: SCM Press.

Part Two

Christmas — Passion — Easter

11

The Nativity Narratives Seen by a Historian

Christian tradition offers the faithful a simple and charming version of the birth of Jesus. It is regularly recounted in Christmas sermons, re-enacted in nativity plays and recreated on the great canvasses of religious art over the centuries.

In the liturgy of the Church the whole Nativity story is squeezed into a shortened time scale between Christmas and Candlemas. Jesus was born in a stable in Bethlehem on 25 December. The innocents were murdered three days later and Jesus was circumcised on New Year's Day. He and his parents visited the Temple on 2 February before journeying to Nazareth. Consequently the flight to and return from Egypt must have taken place between late December and the beginning of February. Everything seems neat and tidy, but is this history or legend?

Our first task is to investigate the sources, i.e. the Infancy Gospels, but even before we turn to Matthew 1—2 and Luke 1—2, 3.23–38, we must delete from the picture the elements devoid of New Testament basis.

The date of the Nativity was first placed by the Western church on 25 December in the fourth century, in a Roman calendar of 334 CE, when Christmas supplanted the pagan festival of the unvanquished sun. But most Eastern Christians celebrated Jesus' birth on the feast of Epiphany, while other oriental communities observed it on 21 April or 20 May.[1] The familiar figure of an elderly Joseph derives from the apocryphal Protoevangelium of James, dating to the second century, which describes him as a widower with sons and daughters from a previous marriage. Neither of the Infancy Gospels includes any allusion to an ox and an ass sharing the stable with Jesus. The imagery is borrowed from Isaiah 1.3. Finally the New Testament nowhere suggests that the oriental visitors who followed the star were kings or that there were three of them. The Greek text of Matthew designates them as *magoi*, 'Magi', magicians or astrologers and the figure of three is no doubt deduced from the mention of the gifts, 'gold and frankincense and myrrh' (Matt. 2.11).

Only the Gospels of Matthew and Luke include infancy narratives. Mark, the earliest of the evangelists, starts his account with John the Baptist baptizing Jesus, and the latest Gospel, that of John, in its mystical prologue outlines the pre-existence of the divine Word (*Logos*) that briefly became incarnate in the person of Jesus. The tales of Matthew and Luke are largely independent from one another and, apart from a few common features, offer different, and occasionally irreconcilable pictures.

Matthew's Account

Matthew's infancy narrative begins with a family tree intended to demonstrate the messianic pedigree of Jesus through his descent via Joseph from King David. The drama opens with Joseph's plan to divorce Mary on discovering that she was pregnant, but his dilemma is resolved by a dream in which an angel attributes his fiancée's condition, not to infidelity, but to the miraculous action of the Holy Spirit. The perturbed Joseph gives credence to this dream-revelation, marries his betrothed but abstains from 'knowing' her until the birth of Jesus.

The birth of Jesus is marked by the apparition of a star on the eastern horizon, which leads the 'wise men' (Magi) of the Orient to Jerusalem. Herod, whom they approach, consults the Jewish chief priests who identify Bethlehem as the predicted birthplace of the Messiah. The king gives the Magi the relevant information and cannily asks them to share with him whatever they learn about the child, but, having found Jesus, the visitors are instructed in a dream to return home without revisiting Herod.

Meanwhile Joseph is ordered by an angel, in yet another dream, to rush Jesus and his mother to Egypt. They thus escape the massacre of the children of Bethlehem decreed by Herod intent on eliminating a royal pretender. On the death of the king the same angel, in a penultimate dream, commands Joseph to go back to the land of Israel. However, a final dream directs him not to return to his home in Bethlehem, now ruled by Archelaus, Herod's son, but take up residence in Nazareth.

Luke's Account

Luke's gentle version of the Nativity contains no dramatic turns. It begins with two annunciations. In the first, the elderly Judaean priest Zechariah is told by the angel Gabriel that his aged and sterile wife Elizabeth will miraculously give birth to John the Baptist. Next, the same Gabriel informs Mary, a virgin from Nazareth engaged to Joseph, and a relative of Elizabeth, that she will conceive Jesus. The baffled girl, who cannot see how this could happen as she is not yet married, is told that it is just as easy for God to make her pregnant while still a virgin as to allow her post-menopausal kinswoman to conceive. Mary visits Elizabeth in Judaea, and soon is on the road again, accompanying Joseph from Nazareth to Bethlehem, his ancestral city, where by virtue of the census ordered by Augustus he has to register. Jesus is born in Bethlehem, in an animal shelter, and is greeted by local shepherds and a heavenly choir. Eight days later, he is circumcised, and on the fortieth day following his birth he is taken to the Temple where the ceremony of the redemption of the firstborn and the mother's purification ritual are performed. From Jerusalem they immediately return to Nazareth, their original hometown.

Comparison between Matthew and Luke

Matthew and Luke agree on the following:

1 The substance of the genealogies. Although the two family trees differ in detail: from Zerubbabel in the late sixth century BCE to Joseph all the ancestors of Jesus bear different names in the two lists, unless Matthan and Matthat are taken to be mere

spelling variations, but both genealogies are meant to prove that Jesus comes from the house of David.

2 The identity of the parents, Mary and Joseph.
3 Some miraculous part played by the Holy Spirit in the conception of Jesus.
4 Bethlehem as the place of birth.
5 Nazareth as the permanent residence of Jesus and his parents.

Differences between Matthew and Luke are as follows:

1 In Matthew the original home of Joseph and Mary is implied to be Bethlehem as no travel is mentioned prior to the flight to Egypt. In Luke, the parents come from Nazareth.
2 In Matthew, not in Luke, Joseph intends to divorce Mary on discovering her pregnancy.
3 Matthew has no knowledge of an imperial census, while Luke cites it as the reason of the journey of Joseph and Mary to Bethlehem.
4 In Luke Jesus is greeted in the stable by angels, shepherds and local people, while in Matthew he is worshipped by the Magi.
5 Matthew, not Luke, refers to the appearance of a miraculous star.
6 Luke, not Matthew, recounts the circumcision of Jesus and his presentation in the Temple.
7 Matthew reports, while Luke is silent on, the meeting of the Magi with Herod, the massacre of the infants in Bethlehem, the escape to Egypt, and the return of the family to Judaea.

Historical Evaluation

The historical evaluation of the birth narratives must start with the examination of the nature of the Infancy Gospels. They represent a specific genre in ancient writings in general and in Jewish literature (biblical and post-biblical) in particular. The conception and life of heroes in classical works and those of several Hebrew patriarchs (Isaac, Jacob, Joseph) and prophets (Moses, Samuel) carry in the Bible the marks of divine intervention. Leaving aside the sons and daughters of Olympian gods and mortal women, classical sources attribute divine paternity to Plato (by Apollo),[2] to Alexander the Great (by Zeus),[3] or even to Jesus' contemporary, the emperor Augustus (again by Apollo).[4] On the Jewish side, Isaac, Jacob, the patriarch Joseph and the prophet Samuel were believed to have been born of barren mothers whose womb was miraculously opened by God (Gen. 18.11–12; 21.1; 25.21–4; 29.31; 1 Sam. 1.1–20). It is reasonable, therefore, to expect similar miraculous features in the infancy story of Jesus, portrayed by both Matthew and Luke as Son of David and Son of God (Matt. 1.1, 23; Luke 1.32). A careful analysis of both birth narratives makes it unquestionably clear that they have been added to the main life story of Jesus. For whereas the infancy accounts echo the principal themes of the main Gospel – the messianic character of Jesus and his specific closeness to God – none of the particular features of the Nativity stories (virginal conception, imperial census, the star and the Magi, Herod's murder plot, flight to and return from Egypt) is as much as alluded to in any of the records of the public life of Jesus.

Special Examination of the Main Problems

It is best to start the examination of the basic data of the Infancy Gospels with two factual elements, the date and place of the birth of Jesus.

The date of birth

Neither evangelist states the precise moment of the Nativity, so we must proceed by inference. Matthew 2.1 places Jesus' birth 'in the days of Herod the King', who reigned from 37 to 4 BCE. The return of the holy family from Egypt and their migration to Galilee are set immediately after the death of Herod (4 BCE) and following the accession of Archelaus, who was in power from 4 BCE to 6 CE (Matt. 2.9, 22). Luke, in turn, dates the conception of John the Baptist, which happened according to him a few months before that of Jesus, to 'the days of Herod, king of Judaea' (Luke 1.5). He also notes that Jesus was 'about thirty years of age' at the time of his baptism by John, in the fifteenth year of Tiberius in 29 CE (Luke 3.23). So we can surmise that the Nativity occurred some time before the spring of 4 BCE. Luke's reference to the universal census decreed by Augustus and implemented in Judaea by the governor of Syria, Quirinius, turns out to be useless since there is no evidence that such a census occurred in the kingdom of Herod, a client king exempt from censuses, or could have been executed by Quirinius, who was not governor of Syria while Herod lived.[5] Luke, in fact, antedates the tax registration enacted by Quirinius in the former territory of Archelaus in 6 CE, ten years after the death of Herod.[6] The approximate dating (some time before 4 BCE) is further supported indirectly by the date of the crucifixion of Jesus under the governorship of Pilate (26–36 CE) and the high priesthood of Caiaphas (19–36 CE).[7]

The place of birth

Both Matthew and Luke firmly assert that Jesus was born in Bethlehem. Matthew attests this both as a fact (2.1) and as the realization of an Old Testament prophecy (Micah 5.2 in Matt. 2.5–6). He voices a view which was common Jewish tradition, namely that the King Messiah would arise from 'the royal city of Bethlehem of Judah'.[8] Luke, as usual, abstains from using a biblical proof text. Instead, he advances an otherwise unknown and basically unlikely rule whereby the registration of the inhabitants of a Roman province had to take place, not in the fiscal office situated in their residential district, but in the city of their remote tribal ancestor, supposedly Bethlehem in the case of Joseph 'because he was of the house and the lineage of David' (Luke 2.4).[9]

Since birth in Bethlehem was a theological necessity for anyone to be acknowledged as the Jewish Messiah, the historical reliability of the testimony of the Infancy Gospels in this regard cannot be taken for granted. In fact, the main Gospels, distinct from the infancy narratives, contain elements that undermine their claim. According to the Synoptic evangelists Jesus was regarded by his contemporaries as a Galilean. Nazareth and the region of the Lake of Gennesaret were his *patris*, a term that can equally mean his hometown, his home country or his birthplace (Mark 6.4; Matt. 13.57; Luke 4.24; John 1.46). Not only was he known as 'the prophet Jesus from Nazareth in Galilee' (Matt. 21.11), but according to the Gospel of John 7.41–2, his countrymen refused to see him as the Messiah on the grounds that he did *not* originate 'from Bethlehem, the village where David was'. In short, Jesus' birth in Bethlehem is asserted with theological certainty, but is queried apparently on the basis of factual knowledge.

The star

Extraordinary astral phenomena regularly appear in Jewish and classical literary sources as signs heralding the birth of illustrious individuals. Matthew's reference to the star leading the Magi to Bethlehem must not therefore be automatically presumed to be a real astronomical phenomenon whose date can be established by scientific means. Over the years an odd medley of theories has been proposed identifying Matthew's star as a supernova, or Halley's comet, or the conjunction of Jupiter and Saturn. None of these explications would be very convincing even if one believed that the Gospels dealt here with astronomical reality. But a star that could be followed first from the East to Jerusalem, then for a few miles further to Bethlehem, where it signalled precisely the house where Jesus resided hardly belongs to the realm of science.

Classical literature close to the time of Matthew's Gospel testifies to the popular belief that the birth of an important personality is always marked by the apparition of a new star.[10] We also know that a few months before the birth of the future emperor Augustus a celestial portent forewarned the Roman senate about the advent of a king.[11] However, the Matthean story was most probably built on an Old Testament story concerning a star arising from Jacob. Numbers 24.17 was interpreted both by Jews and by Christians as alluding to the Messiah. In the light of this prediction Rabbi Akiba proclaimed Simeon ben Kosiba, the leader of the second Jewish revolt against Rome (132–5 CE) to be the Messiah.[12] In turn the greatest Bible interpreter of the ancient Church, Origen of Alexandria (c.185–254 CE) eloquently states apropos of Jesus: 'It is said that from Balaam arose the caste . . . of the Magi . . . They had in their possession . . . all that Balaam had prophesied, including "A star shall come forth from Jacob and a man shall rise from Israel". The Magi held these writings among themselves. Consequently when Jesus was born, they recognized the star and understood that the prophecy had come to fulfilment.'[13] Put plainly, the star of Bethlehem should be the subject of biblical exegesis rather than that of astronomy.

The murder plot

There is nothing unlikely in Matthew's story of Herod ordering the extermination of the infants of Bethlehem to ensure the removal of a potential rival. Flavius Josephus provides a long list of Herod's victims, including Mariamme, his beloved wife, three of his own sons and many others. Nevertheless, the massacre of the innocents points to post-biblical tradition and calls to mind a story well attested in Jewish literature contemporaneous with the Gospels. It relates to the childhood of Moses and more precisely to the decision of Pharaoh to destroy the newborn sons of the Israelites on receiving from his experts and dream interpreters information about the birth of a Jewish boy destined to annihilate the Egyptians and bring salvation to Israel.[14]

When we weigh up the similarities between the Moses-Jesus and Pharaoh-Herod features, their parallelism strikes as compelling and makes one conclude that the Matthean episode was modelled on a tale with which both Palestinian and Diaspora Jews of the age of Jesus were familiar. Its formation was further assisted by Herod's reputation as a bloodthirsty tyrant, capable of indescribable acts of savagery.

The virginal conception

The final and no doubt the most tantalizing problem raised by the Infancy Gospels concerns the conception of Jesus. Did Mary's pregnancy come about without the intervention of a human father or was Jesus Joseph's son?

Although the main Gospel account which deals with the adult Jesus never refers to a miraculous birth, both infancy narratives appear to imply that Joseph had nothing to do with the conception of Jesus. The infancy narratives let their readers believe that the conception of Jesus was even more extraordinary than the divinely assisted pregnancy of the 90-year-old Sarah, of the barren Hannah, mother of Samuel, or of the elderly and sterile Elizabeth. In Matthew, Joseph is told by an angel in a dream that his fiancée's child was produced by the Holy Spirit. In Luke it was Mary who learned from an angel that the divine power would make her conceive the Son of God.

The issue is complex and we can consider here only its most essential aspects.[15] According to Matthew, Mary's pregnancy 'of the Holy Spirit' would realize the words of Isaiah 7.14, 'Behold, a *virgin* shall conceive and bear a son, and his name shall be Emmanuel'. The proof, impressive in appearance, contains a snag: it works only in Greek, the version in which the Gospel of Matthew has survived. However the original Nativity tradition was handed down among Palestinian Jews in Aramaic or Hebrew and for them Isaiah would have been quoted in Hebrew. But the Hebrew Old Testament speaks of a 'young woman' ('*almah*) and not of a virgin (*betulah*), a fact that would render the statement unsuitable as a reference to a virginal conception.

The ensuing implication is that the Matthean virgin birth of Jesus, based on Isaiah's prophecy, cannot be part of the primary Gospel tradition that circulated among Palestinian Jews. The idea derives from the editor of the 'Greek' Matthew, who used the Septuagint's loose rendering of '*almah* not as *neanis* (young woman) but as *parthenos* to scripturally insinuate the virginal conception of Jesus.[16]

The evidence yielded by ancient Jewish Christianity makes plain the Hellenistic slant of Matthew's phrase. Indeed, the Ebionites held that Jesus was conceived through normal sexual union between Joseph and Mary.[17] The same idea underlies the logic of the genealogy of Jesus in Matthew (and in Luke) since his legitimate messianic descent depends on his being *begotten* by Joseph. The introduction of the idea of the virgin birth constrained the writer of Matthew's genealogy, when he came to Jesus, to alter the standard formula, A begat B, B begat C, and substitute for it 'and Jacob begat Joseph, the husband of Mary of whom was born (or begotten) Jesus' (Matt. 1.16), in order to avoid a direct assertion that Joseph was Jesus' father. However, the editorial modification was not complete and some Greek manuscripts as well as the Old Latin and an early Syriac translation of the passage preserve the reading, 'Joseph, to whom the virgin Mary was betrothed, *begat* Jesus'.[18]

Conclusion

The birth stories do not constitute the stuff out of which history is made. However they contain some basic facts. They testify to the birth of a Jewish child by the name of Jesus (*Yeshua* in Hebrew) to a couple called Mary (Miriam) and Joseph, born close to the end the reign of Herod the Great, some time before the spring of 4 BCE. Bethlehem as Jesus' place of birth, though firmly asserted on theological grounds in the Infancy Gospels, is contradicted both by John and by the Synoptic evangelists who prefer Galilee and Nazareth as Jesus' home country and native town.

In the main Christian tradition, the paternity of Jesus is ascribed to God through the action of the Holy Spirit, but some New Testament manuscripts as well as the teaching of the Judaeo-Christian Ebionites point to Joseph as the biological father of Jesus.

While some elements of history may be concealed under the wrappings, the Infancy Gospels abound in legendary characteristics: angels, dreams, virginal conception, miraculous star, etc. For the historian they represent a colourful prologue, prefixed to a theologically inspired biography of Jesus to which is attached an even more majestic epilogue, the resurrection of Jesus.

Notes

1   Clement of Alexandria (c. 150–215), *Stromateis* (Miscellanea) 1.21.

2   Origen, *Against Celsus* 6.8.

3 Plutarch, *Life of Alexander* 3.1.

4 Suetonius, *Augustus* 94.

5 See E. Schürer, G. Vermes and F. Millar, 1973, *The History of the Jewish People in the Age of Jesus Christ*, vol. I, Edinburgh: T.&T. Clark, pp. 399–427.

6 Ronald Syme, 1972, 'The Titulus Tiburtinus', *Vestigia*, Beiträge zur Alten Geschichte 17, Munich: de Gruyter, p. 600.

7 For the reasons for dating the crucifixion on Friday 7 April CE 30, see G. Vermes, 2005, *The Passion*, London: Penguin, pp. 115–16.

8 See Palestinian Talmud, Berakhot 5a.

9 See E. Schürer, G. Vermes and F. Millar, *op. cit.*, pp. 411–3.

10 Pliny the Elder, *Natural History* 2.28.

11 Suetonius, *Augustus* 94.

12 Palestinian Talmud, Taanit 68d.

13 *Homily on the Book of Numbers* 13.7.

14 Josephus, *Jewish Antiquities* 2.205; Targum Pseudo-Jonathan on Exod. 1.15.

15 For a fuller treatment see G. Vermes, 2006, *The Nativity*, London: Penguin, chapter 5.

16 It is to be stressed that in Hebrew *'almah* is not equivalent of virgin, and that even in Greek *parthenos* can designate any unmarried young woman, virgin or not.

17 Eusebius, Ecclesiastical *History* 3.27.

18 An ancient Jewish gossip, devoid of historical credentials, claims that Jesus was born out of wedlock, the son of Mary and a man called Pandera, Pantera or Panthera, possibly a Roman soldier. See Origen, *Against Celsus* 1.28, 32; Babylonian Talmud, Shabbat 104b; cf. recently James D. Tabor, 2006, *The Jesus Dynasty*, New York: Simon & Schuster, pp. 63–72.

12

Matthew's Nativity Is Charming and Frightening . . . But It's a Jewish Myth

When we speak of the Nativity story, we speak, in essence, of the account in St Matthew's Gospel. The virgin birth, Joseph's dream, the star, the Wise Men and their gifts, the flight to Egypt, and Herod's slaughter of the innocents: all these elements are drawn from Chapters 1 and 2 of the first Gospel. Only the adoration of the shepherds and the birth in the manger are missing – these staples of the tale being supplied by St Luke.

St Matthew's account of the Christmas story, like a child's fairy tale, consists of an admixture of the charming and the frightening. The sweet image of the baby cared for by the Virgin Mary, greeted by angels, and visited by the Magi – magicians in pursuit of a miraculous star – is followed by menace. The bloodthirsty Herod enters the fray, informed of Jesus' birth by the Magi, and advised by the interpreters of what we have come to call the Old Testament ('the chief priests and scribes'), sages who identify the place where the new king of Israel is to be found.

To rid himself of a potential rival, Herod lets loose his cruel soldiers on the infants of Bethlehem. They all perish – except the child whom Herod actually fears. Joseph, warned by a dream, carries Jesus to safety in Egypt – where, centuries before, the very existence of the Jewish people had nearly been brought to an end by Pharaoh. Yet another dream, and Joseph is told by 'an angel of the Lord' that he can take Mary and Jesus back to the Holy Land.

This account of Jesus' birth is missing entirely from the Gospels of Mark and John, and appears in a radically different form in Luke, where there is no mention of a star, wise men or Herod, nor of the murder of the innocents and Jesus' escape to Egypt. The question, then, is: what are the true origins of St Matthew's account, which have proved so extraordinarily influential in Christian civilization?

To answer this, we have to examine biblical sources and Jewish folklore. Dreams, for instance, play an essential part in Matthew's account of the Nativity. Joseph discovers by means of a vision that the pregnancy of Mary is miraculous – 'that which is conceived in her is of the Holy Ghost' – in fulfilment of a prophecy by Isaiah.

According to the prophet, a child called 'Emmanuel' would be born of a virgin. The crucial point here is that Matthew is quoting the Greek translation of Isaiah: 'Behold a *parthenos* [virgin] shall conceive and bear a son and shall call his name Emmanuel.' But Isaiah wrote in Hebrew, not in Greek, and in the Hebrew Bible, the mother of Emmanuel is not a virgin – the Hebrew for this would be *betulah* – but a young woman, *almah*, already pregnant. She is to give birth to a son, *Immanu El*, meaning 'God is with us'.

Here, the historical context of Isaiah's original words is key: this name – *Immanu El* – promised divine protection to the inhabitants of Jerusalem during the siege of the city by two enemy kings seven centuries before the birth of Jesus. But the writer responsible for St Matthew's Gospel – which is in Greek – added his own double twist to the Hebrew words of Isaiah, distorting them dramatically in the process. The Gospel author took the translated word *parthenos*, not in the loose sense of a young girl but strictly as 'virgin'; and the name 'God is with us' not as a promise of hope but, literally, as a person sharing the nature of the Deity.

It is hard to exaggerate the significance of these changes. Matthew's Gospel was written in about 80–90 CE for Christians who were not of Jewish provenance – that is, Gentiles who had no knowledge of Isaiah's original Hebrew. For them, the passage announced, unambiguously, the fulfilment of an ancient prophecy: the miraculous birth of a divine being. But the prophet himself and readers of his original Hebrew sentence regarded it as a quite specific allusion to the historical circumstances of Isaiah's age – and would have found its mutation in Greek into one of the foundations of Christian doctrine quite baffling.

Matthew's Christmas narrative also refers to the providential escape of Jesus from Herod's murder plot. Here, the Evangelist did not need to cite biblical authorities such as Isaiah. Herod's record of atrocities was a matter of common knowledge. He was responsible for putting to death his favourite wife, three of his sons, his brother-in-law, his uncle, as well as his mother-in-law and her father, together with countless other Jews. He was certainly capable of murdering small children.

This part of the story is historically plausible, therefore. However, there are good reasons, based on close analysis of Jewish tradition, to suppose that St Matthew's claim is a variant on a powerful tradition rather than a literal historical claim: a generic story, so to speak, rather than a specific one.

A contemporary of Matthew, the Jewish historian Flavius Josephus (37–c.100 CE), reports, and later rabbinic literature confirms, a folk tale which was in circulation in New Testament times. It relates to the birth of Moses and his miraculous escape from the hands of Pharaoh of Egypt. In the Old Testament, the extermination of the new-born male children of the Jews was decreed by the Egyptian king in order to stop the growth of the dissatisfied Jewish population, perceived as a threat to the Egyptian state.

The rabbis recorded a similarly murderous plan. Pharaoh – like Joseph in St Matthew's Gospel – had a dream. In it, he saw two scales, with the whole of Egypt lying in one of them, and a lamb in the other. But the lamb turned out to be weightier than Egypt. The court magicians were summoned and explained to the king that the lamb symbolized a Jewish boy who would become a lethal threat to Egypt. In Aramaic, the word *talya*, like 'kid' in English, can mean both a young animal and a child.

Amram, the father of Moses, also had a dream and learned that his son was the future redeemer of the Jews. Afraid of breaking the royal command, yet intent on saving his son, he constructed a papyrus basket and entrusted the fate of the child to God. As in the Bible, little Moses is said to have been found by Pharaoh's daughter who persuaded her father to appoint Moses as his heir. The willing Pharaoh took the baby in his arms, but Moses grabbed the king's crown and threw it to the floor. The sacred scribe, who had foretold the birth of the liberator of the Jews, realized who the baby was and advised the king to kill him. However, Divine Providence in the person of Pharaoh's daughter quickly stepped in, and Moses survived.

My point is that St Matthew's account of the Nativity – the basis of all Christmas celebrations – appears in a quite different light when it is considered as the product of a particular Jewish linguistic, literary and religious context, rather than the sentimental narrative we have inherited.

The doctrine of the miraculous conception and birth of a God–man was based on a remarkable mistranslation into Greek – willful or otherwise – of Isaiah's original, quite specific Hebrew words. As for the episode of the massacre of the innocents and escape to Egypt, its similarity to the rabbinic story of the birth of Moses is so striking that it hardly can be attributed to coincidence. In both we find dreams, a murderous king advised by interpreters of sacred writings, and the frustration by divine intervention of wicked plans. Nor is it conceivable that Josephus and the rabbis, spokesmen of Jewish tradition, copied their birth legend of Moses from Matthew.

We are led inescapably to this conclusion: that the awesomely influential Nativity story in the first book of the New Testament is a speculative, rather than a historical text. Far from being a report of a literal happening, it is an amalgam of flawed Greek-Christian scriptural references, and of 'birth tales' current in Judaism in the first century CE. The story with which we are all so familiar is not fact, but folklore.

13

Celluloid Brutality

I am still in a state of shock having sat through two hours of almost uninterrupted gratuitous brutality, Mel Gibson's *The Passion of the Christ*. I hope I will never be obliged to see something as dreadful again. Gibson's Jesus is a noble figure and Pontius Pilate a well-intentioned weakling. The Roman soldiers, who do most of the violence, are pictured as sadistic beasts and the Jewish chief priests as self-satisfied smugs who enjoy the humiliation of Jesus. Gibson says his is a correct representation of the Passion and that his movie has been 'directed by the Holy Ghost'.

The crucifixion of Jesus can be considered in three distinct ways.

The theological view is simple. Jesus, the Son of God, sacrificed himself for the sins of mankind and each individual must feel personally guilty for crucifying him. Old-fashioned Christians also hold that the Passion story is to be taken literally from the Last Supper, through the arrest, trial and condemnation of Jesus for blasphemy, to his handing over by the Jewish high court to the Romans on a charge of rebellion. The Jews and Caiaphas, their high priest, appear the villains of the story. They take upon themselves and on their children the blame for killing the Son of God. The doctrine of deicide, into which the traditional perception of the Passion story twisted itself, is considered the chief source of Christian anti-Judaism.

Leaving aside these non-scholarly approaches, how do the New Testament accounts of the last day of Jesus appear in the light of Jewish and Roman history of the first century? Examined with expert eyes, basic questions arise concerning the purpose of the narratives, the identity of the readership for which they were written, and the broader historical setting. To answer these questions the Gospels demand to be interpreted.

The four Gospels do not agree. The traditional picture of the Passion, which underlies the film, has resulted from a selective reading of them. In the first three Gospels, all the events happen on the feast of Passover, a most unlikely situation; in John (with greater probability) on the previous day. In John there is no trial at all, only an interrogation of Jesus by a former high priest, Annas, with no sentence pronounced. By contrast, Mark and Matthew speak of a night session of the Sanhedrin at which Jesus is found guilty of blasphemy by Caiaphas and condemned to death. But a court hearing in a capital case on a feast day is contrary to all known Jewish law. Mark and Matthew refer to a second meeting in the morning, which is the only one alluded to in Luke. In the morning Caiaphas and his court abruptly drop the religious charge and deliver Jesus to Pilate on a political indictment of rebellion. The Roman penalty for sedition was crucifixion, and Jesus, like thousands of Jews before and after him, died on the cross.

The Gospels postdate the events by 40–80 years. They were all compiled after the fall of Jerusalem in 70 CE. By then the large majority of the readers envisaged by the evangelists were non-Jews. After their revolt against Rome (66–73/4 CE), antipathy towards the Jews grew in the Roman Empire, and this affected the depiction of Jesus for new non-Jewish Christians. To admit to them that Rome was fully to blame for the death of the crucified Jewish Christ would have made the fresh converts politically suspect. Christians were an unpopular sect. Hence outside Palestine the Gentile–Christian spin doctors moved in and played down the Jewishness of Jesus and his original disciples. He and his apostles were no longer considered as Jews.

We find also an obvious effort to exonerate Pilate. The New Testament portrait of a vacillating governor of Judea is totally at odds with the historical truth. The real Pilate could not be bullied by the Jewish high priest. He was his boss and could sack him at will. All the reliable first-century sources depict Pilate as a tyrant who was guilty of numerous executions without trial and unlawful massacres. He was justly dismissed from office and banished by the emperor Tiberius.

As for the condemnation of Jesus for blasphemy, no Jewish law would qualify someone a blasphemer simply for calling himself the Messiah or the like. So the death sentence pronounced on Jesus by Caiaphas was an error in law. There are strong arguments in favour of the claim (against John's assertion of the contrary) that first-century Jewish courts could carry out capital sentences for religious crimes without Roman consent. Even Roman citizens risked instant execution if caught by Jews in the Temple.

The abandonment of the case for blasphemy and its replacement by a charge of rebellion is left unexplained in the Synoptic Gospels. But the reasoning that underlies the political accusation is easy to understand. It was the duty of the Jewish leadership, Caiaphas and his council, to maintain order in Judea. Caiaphas imagined that Jesus was a potential threat to peace. Jerusalem, filled with pilgrims at Passover, was a powder keg. A few days earlier, Jesus had created a commotion in the merchants' quarter in the Temple, when he overturned the stalls of the moneychangers. He could do it again. Jesus had to be dealt with in the interest of the whole nation in order to forestall massive Roman retaliation. Caiaphas and his council had the power to punish him, but passed the buck. They therefore bear the blame for surrendering Jesus to the Romans, a fact attested by all four Gospels and confirmed by the first-century Jewish historian Josephus. The Roman writer Tacitus also asserts that Jesus was crucified by the procurator Pontius Pilate. Hence the responsibility for the crucifixion was Pilate's, and ultimately that of the Roman Empire he represented.

So, can the New Testament as such be blamed for fomenting anti-Semitism? A nuanced reply is that its stories about Jesus were not originally conceived as anti-Jewish: they were meant to describe a family row between various Jewish groups. But in non-Jewish surroundings they were liable to receive an anti-Jewish interpretation. Anti-Semitism is not in the New Testament text, but in the eyes and in the minds of some of its readers.

Gibson has repeatedly asserted that neither he, nor his film, is anti-Semitic. The real problem is not with his attitudes or avowed intentions, but with the lack of appropriate steps taken to prevent visual images from inspiring judaeophobia. Caiaphas and his priestly colleagues often struggle not to smile when they see the defeat of Christ. In the film they allow their policemen to beat him up in open court without protest. In the Gospels themselves they are depicted as doing things according to the book and reject the witnesses who testify against Jesus. This does not seem to be so in the film. These are dangerous opportunities for inspiring vengeful sentiments.

The light element in *The Passion of the Christ* is supplied by the use of Latin and Aramaic. Not only are Pilate and Jesus(!) fluent Latin speakers, but even the soldiers of the Jerusalem garrison, who were most probably Aramaic- and Greek-speaking recruits from Syria, converse happily in a clumsy Latin with Italian Church pronunciation. I did not find it easy to follow the Aramaic which was mixed with unnecessary Hebraisms. One point is worth noting. It has been said again and again that the fateful curse 'His blood be on us and our children!' has been cut from the film. This is not so. The Aramaic words are there; only the English subtitle has been removed.

Crucifixion is not a gentle subject: the great Roman orator Cicero calls it *crudelissimum teterrimumque supplicium*, the most cruel and abominable form of death penalty. But Gibson poured into his vision of the Passion of Jesus protracted graphic violence. It inflicts great harm on the noble subject. When written by Shakespeare, the words of Mark Antony describing the blood-soaked mantle of the murdered Julius Caesar and the holes left by the assassins' daggers shake the listener more to the core than the celluloid brutality of *The Passion of the Christ* by Mel Gibson.

14

The Passion

The story of the crucifixion of Jesus has been very much in the news lately thanks to Mel Gibson's Hollywood blockbuster, *The Passion of the Christ*. It was caricatured as the goriest film ever made and as a result of massive protest by sensitive viewers, Gibson consented to shorten his horror movie by six minutes. If I had been entrusted with the cutting, probably only six minutes of the film would have survived. My opposition to it is not based on merely aesthetic grounds, although having sat through the press preview, the more than an hour of uninterrupted gratuitous brutality made me swear that I would never watch something as dreadful again. My chief objection concerns the claim made by the director and his publicists, and swallowed hook, line and sinker by church leaders including apparently the late Pope John Paul II, that the film faithfully reflects the Gospels.

A simplistic and selective reading of the story of the Passion of Jesus in the New Testament has influenced Christian attitudes towards the Jews throughout the centuries. Claiming to represent gospel truth, it confronts us with a vicious Jewish mob and even more vicious priests, determined to get rid of Christ and bulldoze a feeble Pilate into complying with their wicked design. To discover the truth lurking beneath the Passion, one must approach the Gospels under the guidance of historical and literary criticism. We have to take into account the purpose of the narrators, the identity of their readers, and the wider Jewish and Roman contextual evidence.

Since 6 CE, when Judaea was transformed from Herod's kingdom to a Roman province, political issues were dealt with by the tribunal of the Roman governor. But religious offences were in the hands of Jewish courts, the highest of which was the Sanhedrin in Jerusalem, composed of leading priests and lay experts under the presidency the high priest. The gravest crimes, such as idolatry or blasphemy, carried the death penalty according to the Law of Moses. No one could however be condemned unless proved guilty on the concordant testimony of two or three witnesses.

Four methods of execution were practised in Jewish Palestine in the first century BCE and CE: stoning, burning, strangling and beheading. For instance, James the brother of Jesus was stoned by order of the high priest Ananus in 62 CE; some Pharisees were burned alive by King Herod, who also ordered the strangling of two of his sons. The first-century Jewish historian Flavius Josephus reports that John the Baptist was decapitated by Herod Antipas as a potential revolutionary and the same mode of execution awaited the apostle James son of Zebedee by order of the Herodian king Agrippa I according to the Acts of the Apostles.

Crucifixion was apparently practised by Jews in the early first century BCE. The Maccabean priest-king Alexander Jannaeus crucified 800 Pharisee rebels, and the Dead Sea Scrolls list crucifixion as the Jewish penalty for treason. But by the first century CE crucifixion was an exclusively Roman form of death penalty, reserved for foreigners, slaves and revolutionaries. Cicero called it 'the most cruel and abominable mode of execution' – *crudelissimum teterrimumque supplicium*. It was common in Judaea. Varus, the Roman governor of Syria, crucified 2000 Jewish revolutionaries outside Jerusalem in 4 BCE, and during the siege of the city in 70 CE up to 500 captured Jews died on Roman crosses every day.

The story of the Passion of Jesus was recorded two generations after the event. The Gospels were most probably composed in Greek after the fall of Jerusalem in 70 CE roughly between 70 and 110 CE. They addressed a largely non-Jewish readership in Syria, Asia Minor, Greece, Italy and Egypt. After the failed Judaean revolt against Rome (66–70 CE) most of these readers disliked the Jews. The hostile atmosphere influenced the presentation of the life and the death of Jesus. For the evangelists to admit plainly that their

Jewish hero was crucified by the Romans on the charge of sedition would have been counterproductive. In fact, we know from the Latin writers Tacitus and Pliny the Younger that the Christians of the late first and early second century were perceived as members of a criminal and dangerous sect. It is no surprise therefore that for non-Jewish readers outside Palestine the Jewishness of Jesus was diluted. In the eyes of Gentile Christians the Jews were the enemies of Jesus and of the Church. Hence Jesus and his apostles could no longer be recognized as Jews.

Parallel with this growing anti-Judaism, we discern a tendency in the Gospels to exonerate Pilate, and the Romans. Yet the portrait encountered in the New Testament of a vacillating well-meaning weakling is totally at odds with historical reality. First-century Jewish writers, Philo and Josephus, depict him as a lawless and vicious tyrant, responsible during his ten years in office (26–36 CE) for numerous executions without trial and for massacres of Jews and Samaritans. He was not someone to be steamrollered by Caiaphas into crucifying Jesus. The high priests were in the governors' hands: they were appointed by them and could be dismissed at will. In 36 CE Pilate reaped his just deserts. Found guilty of massacring a group of Samaritans, he was sacked by the emperor Tiberius and exiled to Gaul. At the same time Caiaphas was also demoted.

Regarding the trial of Jesus the Gospels contradict one another and some of their assertions are also intrinsically implausible. Before his arrest in Jerusalem, Jesus is depicted as a popular Galilean charismatic teacher, preaching the imminent arrival of the Kingdom of God. Although occasionally criticized by synagogue bigots, multitudes of Jews flocked to him in Galilee bringing the sick to the healing prophet. Even on his entry to Jerusalem a few days before the crucifixion Jesus was cordially welcomed, and the Temple authorities, though suspicious, were afraid to challenge him openly because of his popularity with the crowds. Yet in the same Gospels there was no one to speak up for him in his hour of need.

Inside a week everything went wrong for Jesus in Jerusalem. Outraged by the goings-on in the Temple courtyard, the fiery

Galilean prophet was moved by religious enthusiasm, and caused a commotion by overturning the tables and stalls of the money-changers and merchants of sacrificial animals. Jesus was not a revolutionary but he lived in a revolutionary age and Passover was the Jewish feast of liberation when Jerusalem was filled with pilgrims like Mecca with Muslims on *hajj*. The creation of a tumult in the Temple around Passover was a foolish act in the eyes of the priestly guardians of order who were responsible to the Romans for the keeping of peace. For them Jesus was a *potential* trouble-maker. He came from Galilee, a hotbed of anti-Roman agitation, and some of his disciples, like Simon the Zealot, were suspected to be revolutionaries. Jesus had to be dealt with to avoid another disorder that might provoke massive Roman retaliation.

So the chief priests ordered the detention of Jesus. He was *secretly* apprehended at night and brought before the priestly leaders. The four Gospels give conflicting accounts of his last day, which according to Jewish time reckoning began at dusk and lasted until sunset the next day. Matthew, Mark and Luke place the arrest of Jesus after the Passover dinner in the evening of Thursday, the 15th day of the month of Nisan. His trial by the Sanhedrin of Jerusalem is said to have taken place in the same evening. Witnesses were called against him, but their testimonies did not agree and were rejected in conformity with established court regulations. Finally the high priest Caiaphas challenged Jesus to declare whether he was the Christ, the Son of God, and pronounced him guilty of blasphemy, a crime punishable by death, for claiming, directly or equivocally, to be the Messiah.

But here we have a problem. To become guilty in Jewish law of the capital offence of blasphemy, one had to misuse the sacrosanct name of God, an offence Jesus plainly did not commit. Calling oneself the Messiah, the Son of God, even the glorified Messiah expected to sit on the right hand of God, did not constitute blasphemy unless 'Son of God' was interpreted anachronistically, not in its figurative sense current among Jews in the age of Jesus, meaning someone close to God, but in its much later Christian theological significance of a person sharing the nature of the deity. Moreover, if Caiaphas erroneously thought that Jesus had blasphemed, he should have ordered his execution by stoning in conformity with the Mosaic legislation – which he failed to do.

To complicate matters, after condemning Jesus for blasphemy at night, next morning the court abruptly changed its mind and delivered him to Pilate, not as a blasphemer, but as a revolutionary. Finally, the implausibilities of the Synoptic Gospels reach their climax when contrary to Jewish religious law they claim that the court sat during Passover night and in the morning of Passover day contrary to the express prohibition of such proceedings during Sabbaths and festivals.

The Gospel of John avoids all these pitfalls. Its tradition also places the arrest of Jesus on a Thursday evening, but identifies that day as 14 Nisan, the day *before* Passover. It is silent on the illegal night trial of the Synoptics and substitutes for it an informal interrogation of Jesus by the former high priest Annas in the same evening. In fact, in John there is no Jewish religious trial at all, and Jesus is handed over directly to the Romans next morning. *John's chronology and story line are incontestably preferable.*

Why was the case of Jesus transferred from the Sanhedrin to the tribunal of Pilate? Curiously only John, who speaks of no Jewish trial, addresses this question. According to the tutorial in Roman law given to Pilate by the chief priests, the transfer was necessary because Jewish courts were forbidden by Rome to carry out any death sentence. But both Philo of Alexandria and Flavius Josephus assert the entitlement of Jewish authorities to put to death persons, Jews and non-Jews, including Roman citizens, for a religious offence, namely if they were caught in an area of the Temple which it was forbidden to them to enter. There is no reference to the need of obtaining the Roman governor's consent. If so, the decision of the Sanhedrin to hand over Jesus' case to Pilate did not reflect legal incapacity, but rather an unwillingness to execute him.

If one needs a culprit for the condemnation of Jesus, this is surely not the Jewish people; they cannot be blamed for the crucifixion any more than the British nation as such for the Blair government's decision to attack Iraq. The responsibility for delivering Jesus to the Romans belonged to the priestly authorities and on the high priest in particular. Caiaphas was a shrewd operator with 12 years of experience in diplomatic tightrope walking with the Romans. To stay on the right side of Pilate – and keep his job – he had to show himself a zealous guardian of the peace against potential revolutionaries. He found an excuse for the unpleasant duty of handing over a Jew to the Romans by the thought that this was necessary to protect the interest of the larger community. So he preferred to pass the buck. He bears a large portion of the blame for the fate of Jesus, even though the ultimate *legal* responsibility for the crucifixion belongs to Pilate and to the Roman Empire. In all probability it was a major miscarriage of justice as Jesus does not seem to have been motivated by political ambition.

In the light of these considerations, let's now try to reconstruct the course of events on the last day of the life of Jesus. Adopting John's dating, the last meal of Jesus took place on Thursday evening, the start of 14 Nisan, the day preceding Passover. It was not a Passover meal and John, unlike the other three Gospels, makes no reference to the institution of the Eucharist. Jesus was stealthily arrested by the envoys of the Temple authorities and questioned by the influential former high priest Annas. He sent Jesus over to the house of Caiaphas, no doubt with the recommendation that he should be charged as a suspected revolutionary before the Romans. Consequently, the following morning the Sanhedrin without further ado dispatched Jesus to Pilate.

In considering the case of Jesus, Pilate seems to have decided to make use of the custom (unattested outside the Gospels) of the Passover amnesty, the release of a Jewish prisoner before the festival. One candidate, a certain Barabbas, nowhere else mentioned in the Gospels or outside the New Testament, had already been lined up. A crowd had already gathered outside the palace of Pilate. As they were not brought there by the chief priests, the best surmise is that they were the supporters of Barabbas. When a choice between Barabbas and Jesus was offered by the governor, they naturally asked for their man, and since Jesus' friends had all gone into hiding, no one dared to speak up for him. Nevertheless the Gospels' assertion that a first-century Jerusalem crowd was urging the Romans to crucify a Jew is highly questionable.

So Jesus was crucified at noon and died on the cross three hours later. Mark's terse notice about the solitary agony of Jesus witnessed from a distance only by three brave Galilean women should be preferred to the other versions which all try to improve on it. Matthew speaks of many women; Luke of all the acquaintances of Jesus, and John brings to the cross Jesus' mother, his aunt, his beloved disciple and Mary Magdalene. Jesus was hastily buried before the onset of Passover which in that year was also a Sabbath.

This combination of the Sabbath and Passover, a feast celebrated by the Jews at full moon after the spring equinox, may allow us to fix the date of Jesus' death with the help of historical and astronomical evidence. We know from Luke 3.1 that the ministry of John the Baptist (and of Jesus) began in the fifteenth year of Tiberius, in 29 CE. The most likely length of the public career of Jesus was less than one year with a single Passover mentioned in the Synoptic Gospels. This would place the Passion in the spring of 30 CE. Now according to the best astronomical calculation the spring full moon and the Jewish Passover of 30 CE fell on Saturday, 8 April. So if in conformity with John's calendar reckoning Jesus expired on the cross around 3 p.m. on the eve of Passover before the start of the Sabbath, it most likely happened on Friday, 7 April 30 CE.

15

Caiaphas Was Innocent?

In the storm of publicity which has preceded the release of Mel Gibson's gory film, *The Passion of the Christ*, its promoters have claimed (though the Vatican has denied) that the Pope gave his blessing to the movie saying: 'It is as it was.' This is supposed to mean that the film is historically reliable. Gibson was less reticent and suggested that it was 'directed by the Holy Ghost'. For students of first-century Jewish history, I am afraid things are not that simple.

The Passion story of the New Testament can be seen in three distinct ways. The theological view is that the Son of God sacrificed himself to redeem the sins of all men. Each human being should feel responsible for his death on the cross.

Next we have the literal reading of the Gospel story. There we encounter determined Jews, headed by their high priest Caiaphas, wishing to see Jesus dead, and bullying a weak Roman governor into complying with their design. This understanding of the Gospel account of the Passion was twisted into the doctrine of deicide – the notion that the Jews killed God – and to the deplorable caricature of the Jewish people as Christ-killers. The Second Vatican Council – which Mel Gibson, as an ultra-traditional Catholic, rejects – explicitly condemned and exorcized this devilish teaching.

The objective of the third approach is to uncover the true Passion story lurking beneath the text of the New Testament by determining the purpose of the narrators, the identity of its readers, the wider historical setting and the use of textual interpretation.

The four Gospels were all written after the suppression of the Jewish revolt against Rome between 70 and 110 CE. By the end of the first century the very large majority of the intended readers were non-Jewish inhabitants of the Graeco-Roman world. They shared the prevailing strong anti-Jewish sentiment which followed the unpopular rebellion against the Empire. For the Gospel writers to have advanced the claim that a Jewish Redeemer was crucified by Pilate – that Rome was to blame – would have been wholly counterproductive.

Given this highly specific context, it is no surprise that Jesus and his followers are not really presented as Jews. By contrast, it is the Jews that the Gospels – especially Matthew – blame for the death of Jesus. (In Mark, the chief priests ask for witnesses; in Matthew for false witnesses.) Again, Matthew alone carries the fateful words, 'His blood be on us and on our children' – a curse upon all Jews for the rest of time. Every effort is made, on the other hand, to excuse Pontius Pilate of complicity in the crime, short of denying that it was he who ordered the crucifixion.

About Pilate a great deal is known. All the first-century sources other than the Gospels depict him as a harsh, insensitive and cruel figure, guilty of bribery, and responsible for numerous executions without trial. He was dismissed and banished by the emperor Tiberius. The portrait in the New Testament of a vacillating weakling, troubled by his conscience but eventually yielding to the bloodthirsty Jewish mob, is quite at odds with what we know of the real Pilate.

The governors were also the absolute masters of the Jewish high priests whom they appointed and sacked at will. It is complete historical nonsense, as is apparently implied in Gibson's film, to suggest that Caiaphas bulldozed Pilate into executing Jesus. *The Passion of the Christ* is only the latest version of the story over the centuries to present Caiaphas as the villain of the piece. In fact, he found himself in an unenviable position. As the head of the Jews in Judaea, he and his council were duty-bound to keep law and order for the Romans in a troublesome country and an even more turbulent Jerusalem, filled with crowds of international pilgrims around Passover. For the Jews, Passover was the feast of liberation and the moment of the year when the Messiah was expected to appear. In the powder keg of first-century Jerusalem any disturbance would have provoked violent Roman retaliation.

Jesus was guilty of causing a commotion in the merchants' quarter in the Temple when he overturned the stalls and tables of the dealers in animals and moneychangers. From the point of view of the authorities, he was a dubious charismatic prophet, preaching a new Kingdom of God. He had a following. He and his men were Galileans, and Galilee was a hotbed of anti-Roman agitation. Some of his companions were reputed to be revolutionaries like Simon the Zealot – and maybe even Judas Iscariot, if Iscariot derives from Sicarius, a murderous dagger man. So Jesus had to be dealt with to avoid disorder in which many innocent Jews might have been slaughtered.

According to the Gospel writers, Caiaphas judged Jesus to be a blasphemer for calling himself the Messiah. Such an assertion did not amount to blasphemy in any Jewish law, biblical or post-biblical. But if Caiaphas mistakenly thought it did, he should have condemned him to die by stoning, the prescribed Jewish capital penalty for a religious crime. Yet, having declared him guilty, the court abruptly changed tack. It abandoned the religious charge for a new political one and laid it before Pilate: Jesus was a rebel. Crucifixion was the Roman penalty for sedition and Jesus, like thousands of Jewish revolutionaries, died on the cross.

Here we need to pause and reflect. Why did Caiaphas not order his henchmen to proceed with the stoning of Jesus? The first three Gospels overlook the question. Only John makes the Jews give Pilate a legal tutorial in which they claim to him that they are not authorized to carry out the death penalty. But was this, in fact, the case? There is, it is true, some evidence to show that the right to put a criminal to death was the exclusive privilege of the Roman governor. But there are arguments that appear even stronger suggesting quite otherwise.

There were, it seems, circumstances in which the Jews themselves could impose capital punishment without Rome's permission. Philo of Alexandria, an older contemporary of Jesus, attests that entry into the innermost area of the Temple was punishable by death without appeal. The Jewish historian Josephus (37–c100 CE) and an inscription from the Temple also proclaim that any non-Jew, even a Roman citizen, risked his life if caught inside the sanctuary. In such cases, there was no need for the Roman governor's consent. We also learn from the Acts of the Apostles that when St Paul was summoned before the Sanhedrin (the Supreme Court in Jerusalem) on a capital charge, he was so afraid of being found guilty and put to death that he used the privilege of a Roman citizen to appeal to the emperor's tribunal.

From all this we can draw an important conclusion: the decision of Caiaphas to hand Jesus' case over to Pontius Pilate did not reflect his legal incapacity to execute him, but his unwillingness to do so. He was passing the buck – and the decision to crucify Jesus was Pilate's and Pilate's alone.

This is not pure speculation. In 62 CE, some 30 years after the crucifixion of Christ, another Jesus, the son of Ananias, was brought before the Jewish high court in Jerusalem on the charge of fomenting disorder during the pilgrimage Feast of Tabernacles. The magistrates first tried to silence him by a severe beating. It did not work, so they handed him over to the Roman governor Albinus because they were worried that he might be God's prophet. He administered an even worse beating to the accused before interrogating him. This Jesus refused to reply. But this story has a happier ending than that of Jesus of Nazareth. As Jesus, son of Ananias, was without followers, the governor concluded that he was a lunatic and let him go.

I hope that, seen in their genuine historical context, the New Testament accounts of the trial and execution of Jesus will become less perplexing and less likely to feed anti-Semitism. Perhaps the Pope's alleged verdict of Gibson's film should be reformulated to read: it would be better if it were not.

16

Iscariot and the Dark Path to the Field of Blood

Judas Iscariot, who betrayed Jesus with a perfidious kiss, has been viewed throughout the ages as the chief villain of the story of the Crucifixion.

In January 2006, however, it was rumoured that the Vatican, following revisionist theologians who argued that Judas was simply Jesus' agent in his dealings with the chief priests, was planning to rehabilitate the black sheep among the Apostles.

These rumours turn out to anticipate the main thesis of the apocryphal Gospel of Judas which has just been released, to a blaze of excitable publicity, by the National Geographic Society. It is the product of the Gnostic heresy composed in Greek in the second half of the second century CE, and surviving in a very poorly preserved Coptic translation from the fourth century.

The existence of this Gospel was attested by the Church Father Irenaeus of Lyons (180 CE), who ascribed it to the sect of the Cainites, hero-worshippers of such dark biblical characters as Cain, Esau, Korah and Judas. While the 'new' papyrus may reveal some of the non-Jewish ideas of Greek Gnosticism, it cannot improve the genuine picture of the events of the last days of Jesus. For a more level-headed view of the part played by Judas in these events, we still have to rely on the handful of data contained in the New Testament.

Concerning Judas, the four Gospels and the Acts of the Apostles have three points in common. First, he was one of the 12 apostles. Second, he was instrumental in the arrest of Jesus, singling him out, according to the Synoptic Gospels, in the dark orchard of Gethsemane by what has become known as the Judas kiss. Incidentally this embrace did not necessarily indicate love or close friendship. It was a social custom. Jewish hosts greeted their guests, and members of the early Christian churches each other, with a kiss.

Third, a financial motive stands behind the act of Judas. In Mark and Luke the chief priests offered him a bribe, but in Matthew it was Judas who demanded to be paid. John in turn, without mentioning a deal, describes Judas, the treasurer of the apostles, as an embezzler who stole from the common kitty. The precise sum of 30 pieces of silver appears only in Matthew, who, as customary, draws on the Old Testament, here on two prophecies (Zech. 11.13 and Jer. 23.7–9), wholly irrelevant to the story of Jesus.

We have two contradictory accounts of Judas' death. In Matthew he seems to have expected Jesus somehow to extricate himself, as he was wont to do, from the plight in which Judas had placed him. On realizing, however, that this was not to be the case, he broke down and decided to return the blood money, but as the chief priests refused to take it back, let alone to change their plans, he hanged himself. The money was then used by the Temple authorities to buy a plot of land, the Field of Blood, for the burial of strangers.

In Luke's account, far from repenting, Judas purchases a field with the money but, while visiting it, he suffers a fatal accident. The death of Judas was used in popular Christian circles to explain the Aramaic place name, Akeldama, Field of Blood. In Matthew it is so called because it was purchased with blood money; but in Acts the designation signals that the traitor's blood was spilt on it.

While Luke and John attribute the downfall of Judas to the influence of the Devil, some recent writers try to portray him in more favourable colours. The linguistic argument claims that the Greek word 'to hand over' (*paradidômi*) is erroneously rendered in English as 'to betray'. It is suggested by one apologist for Judas that his task was merely to 'make a connection' between Jesus and the chief priests. But there was no need for a go-between to arrange such a meeting since Jesus could be found every day teaching in the Sanctuary. In fact an encounter had already taken place there between him and a delegation of chief priests, scribes and elders shortly after the commotion caused by Jesus in the merchants' quarter of the Temple, but this further exacerbated the situation (Mark 11.27; Matt.21.23; Luke 20.1).

To grasp the true meaning of the concept 'to hand over' in a first-century CE Palestinian Jewish context, it is enough to realize that the Greek word corresponds to the Hebrew term *masar*, used in rabbinic literature to designate a Jew delivering another Jew into the hands of the ruling power.

In anti-Roman Judaea such an act was betrayal and its perpetrator was a despicable collaborator. When Luke (6.16) refers to Judas as a *prodotês* or 'traitor', instead of using the more subtle 'he who handed him over' (Matt. 10.4; Mark 3.19), he simply calls a spade a spade. It is a red herring to maintain that 'betraying' is a mistranslation. In the story of Judas, 'handing over' always carries a pejorative overtone.

Some of the theological arguments are, to put it mildly, purely speculative, such as: 'If God decided to deliver Christ to the chief priests, Judas cannot be blamed for it' or 'If Jesus possessed prescience, he must have known and willed the future conduct of Judas, betrayal included.' Such reasoning cuts no ice with the historically minded.

Other theologians seek to combine speculative thought with their own reading of the New Testament. Their chief argument lies in the words Jesus addressed to Judas in John's version of the Last Supper: 'What you are going to do, do quickly' (John 13.27). They read into these, anticipating the new Gnostic gospel, an instruction to Judas to pour oil on troubled waters between Jesus and the chief priests.

But there is no supporting evidence in the Gospels that Jesus sought an accommodation with the Temple authorities. Moreover, such an understanding of the saying is patently contradicted by the preceding passage in John (and in the other Gospels) in which Jesus predicts that one of his Apostles would hand him over to his enemies (John 13.21; Mark 14.18; Matt. 16.21; Luke 22.21).

Put in colloquial language, 'What you are going to do, do quickly.' amounts to 'I know what you are up to. What holds you back?' The evangelist dramatically concludes: 'He immediately went out and it was night' (John 13.30).

Far from requiring a fundamental reassessment, the historicity of Judas' role, as attested in the New Testament, must be recognized as the linchpin without which the Passion story would fall apart. In the Gospels the chief priests, fearful of popular outrage at any heavy-handed action against Jesus, decided to postpone his arrest until after Passover: 'Not during the feast, lest there be a tumult of the people' (Mark 14.2; Matt. 26.5; Luke 22.2). However, Judas' unexpected move offered a chance to arrest Jesus without witnesses. They seized the opportunity and sent in their troops in the dead of night.

17

The Resurrection

The resurrection of Jesus lies at the heart of the message of Christianity. The chief herald of this message, St Paul, bluntly proclaims: 'If Christ has not been raised, your faith is futile.' How does his firm statement, reinforced by two millennia of theological cogitation, compare with what the Gospels tell us about the first Easter? Is it pure myth or does it contain also a grain of history?

To begin with, resurrection was neither an old, nor a widespread Jewish doctrine in the age of Jesus. The concept of afterlife, conceived either as spiritual survival or as rising from the dead, first gained prominence in the second century BCE. The immortality of the soul was championed by many Jews living outside the Holy Land and influenced by Greek culture as well as by the Essene sect in Palestine according to the first-century Jewish historian Flavius Josephus. The conservative Sadducees and their high-priestly allies considered the idea of life after death a departure from biblical faith where reward for virtue and punishment for sin were expected in this life. Beyond the grave everybody shared the same chilly and sleepy existence in the Hades of the Hebrews. The principal innovators were the Pharisees; they promoted the doctrine of resurrection among urban Jewry. But the bulk of the rural population was mostly confused. Resurrection rarely figures on tomb inscriptions.

Turning to the Gospels, resurrection is not among the central tenets of the teaching of Jesus; he was more concerned with eternal life than with the revival of dry bones. One may also put a question mark to his repeated announcements of his death and resurrection. The fact that all his disciples abandoned him when he was arrested and no one expected his rising suggests that these prophecies did not originate with Jesus, but were added later. We find no apostle comforting himself on Good Friday: Let's wait three days and all will be well.

Belief in the resurrection of Jesus consists in two combined sets of stories about an empty tomb and a series of apparitions. All four Gospels report that the body of Jesus was missing from the grave when one or several women visited it early on Easter Sunday. The idea of resurrection comes from one or two unknown men presumed to be angels who met the women in the tomb (Mark, Matt. and Luke). By contrast, in John, Mary Magdalene suspects that Jesus' remains were removed by someone not connected with the apostles. She asked the unknown man standing close by, later identified as Jesus, where he put the missing body. At the end, the argument is seriously weakened by the apostles' rejection of the women's report which they ridiculed as an 'idle tale'.

The second type of 'evidence', the apparitions of the risen Jesus to his apostles, does not fare much better either. The oldest account, Mark 16.1–8 (the inauthentic verses 9–20 are missing from the best manuscripts) contains no visions at all. According to Luke and John, Jesus was seen by the apostles in Jerusalem on Easter Sunday and Luke mentions an encounter with two disciples on the same day some miles away in Emmaus. Matthew in turn places the only meeting of Jesus with 11 apostles days later on a Galilean mountain, and John asserts that seven apostles saw him by the Sea of Tiberias. To muddle the story further, Luke's Jesus orders his disciples not to leave Jerusalem at all until Pentecost. As for the identity of the appearing person, Mary Magdalene took him for the gardener, the Emmaus disciples for an unknown passer-by and the Jerusalem apostles for a ghost.

There are four rational ways for explaining away the resurrection conundrum.

1 The body was not found by the women because the guardian of the cemetery used the first opportunity to move the body of Jesus out of the grave which had been prepared for someone else.
2 In the darkness the women lost their way and went to a wrong tomb. The uncertainty in both cases could have been easily dis-

pelled by consulting the owner of the tomb, Jesus' friend, Joseph of Arimathea, but no one seems to have thought of it.

3 The apostles stole the corpse as was alleged by the priestly leaders. But since nobody expected Jesus to rise again, why should anybody fake his resurrection?

4 Jesus was buried alive and later woke up and left to live happily for a time if not ever after. This modern concoction, popularized by *The Da Vinci Code*, is unsupported by ancient evidence, though we know that recovery from crucifixion was possible. Flavius Josephus mentions that three of his friends were taken off the cross in 70 CE and were attended by Roman physicians and that one of them survived. In this class of literature, Jesus usually marries Mary Magdalene and settles somewhere away from Judaea, in the south of France or in Rome, but according to the nineteenth century Islamic sect of the Ahmadiyya, he journeyed instead to the East in search of lost Jewish tribes and died in India.

Neither positive nor negative reasoning leads anywhere because the resurrection of Jesus cannot be compared to events belonging to history. There is however one phenomenon that may lead us out of this maze: the transformation of the apostles. It was not due to the apparitions of Jesus. They remained frightened and continued to hide for another seven weeks after Easter. What catapulted them into action was Pentecost, the metamorphosis achieved by the inward experience of the Spirit. Pusillanimous men became spiritual warriors. The charismatic potency imparted to them by Jesus during his ministry and the recollection of his powerful teaching resulted again in mighty words and deeds. They felt their Master close to them: he rose in their hearts.

This is the historical element in the resurrection saga.

Part Three

The Dead Sea Scrolls

18

Secrets of the Scrolls

The Dead Sea Scrolls have not ceased to fascinate experts and amateurs alike since their discovery by Bedouins and archaeologists in the region of Qumran in the 1940s and '50s.

The chief cause of the excitement was the antiquity of the scrolls, which antedate by a millennium the oldest previously known codices of the complete Hebrew Bible. They also reveal for the first time a whole body of Jewish religious literature traceable roughly to between 200 BCE and 70 CE. Enthusiasm was further sharpened by the scrolls' potential impact on our understanding of nascent Christianity. However, the subsequent history of the scrolls has been one of delay, secrecy and even allegation of scandal.

Despite a century of exploration of the length and breadth of the land of the Bible, archaeologists had failed to unearth a single ancient Hebrew manuscript, when, suddenly between 1947 and 1956, a series of discoveries in 11 caves in the region of Qumran yielded the remains of some 900 writings: a dozen rolls and tens of thousands of fragments. However, initial elation at the discovery gradually gave way to increasing exasperation.

For nearly 40 years, a small editorial team retained complete control over the scroll fragments. Their secretiveness and procrastination became so pronounced that scholars, journalists and many interested laymen began to ask whether the delay in publication was deliberate and intended to hide something. Some speculated that the thousands of manuscript fragments from Cave 4 remained undisclosed because the Roman Catholic priests who made up most of the editorial team believed that the scrolls' contents threatened traditional Christianity.

International pressure for free access to the scrolls came to a head on 22 September 1991, when the Californian Huntington Library unilaterally decided to open its Qumran microfilm collection to all competent scholars. A month later, the editorial team and the Jerusalem Antiquities Authority reluctantly bowed to 'people power' and lifted the embargo they had imposed on three photographic archives outside Israel: two in America and one in Oxford.

So what was the cause of the hold-up? The conspiracy theory can be dismissed for a start. As one who has been acquainted with the scrolls from the outset, and has known all the *dramatis personae*, I totally reject it as a figment of the imagination of some frustrated academics. There is no evidence to support it.

Incompetence can also be discarded as an explanation: most members of the original team were talented scholars, and J. T. Milik, in particular, has demonstrated outstanding gifts in assembling and deciphering what must be one of the world's greatest jigsaw puzzles.

The delay was really caused by the mass of scroll fragments unearthed in Cave 4. The late Father Roland de Vaux, an authoritarian French Dominican in charge of the scrolls, made a double error of judgement. He recruited a team that was too small for the task (half-a-dozen mostly young scholars) and instructed them to issue *definitive* editions. In the preface of one of the volumes the editor speaks of 'sufferings and tears' when obliged to confront 2,057 worthless scraps of papyrus, rejected by all his colleagues.

By the late 1960s a fresh chill was added to an already cooling excitement. Some of the editors resented the Israeli takeover of administration of the scrolls in 1967. Père de Vaux refused to co-operate right up to his death in 1971. The following year, a member of the team, the American Monsignor Patrick Skehan, informed de Vaux's successor, Pierre Benoit, another French Dominican, that he would not allow his name to appear on a publication under Israeli auspices. His dilemma was solved from above, for he died in 1980 without submitting the typescript which he had promised for 1975. Even as late as 1990, in a one-page preface to volume eight of the official series, the third chief editor, John

Strugnell, deliberately avoids any mention of the State of Israel, and refers only to anonymous 'governmental authorities'.

Leaving aside the political implications, the survivors and heirs of the ineffective editorial squad adopted what can be best described as a proprietorial attitude towards the scrolls of which they were trustees. They began in the 1970s to hand over parts of their assignment to doctoral students under their control. Otherwise, the unpublished texts continued to be kept under lock and key, and not even a catalogue was made available. The 25 privately issued copies of a concordance, listing alphabetically the words contained in the fragments, were meant only for the 'elect'.

In short, the monumental mishandling of the Dead Sea Scrolls is attributable to prosaic causes: fundamental misjudgements by Roland de Vaux and his successors, and an unwillingness on the part of the editors to admit openly their inability to honour their grandiose undertakings.

Finally, a brief word on the scrolls and the New Testament. Here the media are guilty of having been too easily taken in by sensation or misguided scholars. Back in 1950, the late André Dupont-Sommer persuaded himself that the Teacher of Righteousness, the chief character of the scrolls, was a Christ before Jesus, one who was put to death, rose and was to be seen again judging his enemies in an eschatological apotheosis. The theory turned out to be based on a mistranslation.

Again, here in Britain, the late John Allegro stole the headlines with his claim that the Teacher of Righteousness was a crucified Messiah. But when the text on which he relied was scrutinized, it became obvious that it was not the Teacher who was crucified, but the political opponents of a Jewish leader, plotting against him in connivance with a Syrian Greek king.

On 9 November 1991, Professor Robert Eisenman was reported uncritically by *The Times* as having found in a five-line Qumran fragment evidence that the community believed in a messianic 'Prince of the Congregation, Branch of David', who was violently put to death. When I carefully checked his theory in the Oxford Centre's Qumran archive, the conclusion became inescapable that Dr Eisenman had misunderstood the text, which is related to the already known War Rule, and speaks not of the Messiah's death, but of the annihilation by him of the forces of darkness.

Given the many genuine links between the Dead Sea Scrolls and the New Testament, who needs imaginary ones, however dramatic? The Qumran community and primitive Jewish Christianity should be viewed as parallel dissident movements springing from first century CE mainstream Judaism. Both believed that their destiny was divinely foreordained and predicted. Both venerated their respective founders as revealers of the ultimate truth. Both claimed to be the true Israel. Both awaited the imminent end of time. Both were beginning to be puzzled by the continued postponement of the Day of the Lord.

19

Exploring the Scrolls

If the proverbial opinion pollster accosted passers-by in London or New York, asking them for a definition of the Dead Sea Scrolls, apart from the don't knows, half of his clients would mutter: 'The Scrolls . . . Hmm . . . Aren't they old religious books kept locked away in the Vatican?' More than 60 years after their discovery in 1947, the Scrolls still have not made their full impact on the general public.

I was enormously privileged to witness from its initial stages the story of the Scrolls and to play an active part in their investigation and in their communication to the world. I first learned about them in 1948, the year after an Arab shepherd accidentally tumbled on seven rolls in a cave by the Dead Sea in Palestine, then under British mandate, not yet divided into Israel and Jordan. I was reading biblical studies in Louvain (Belgium) and keenly followed the press reports about Jewish manuscripts purported to date to the end of the pre-Christian era. The story seemed unbelievable: it flatly contradicted the accepted wisdom according to which no ancient document written on leather could survive in the Palestinian climate.

The decisive moment came one sunny morning, still in 1948. My professor of Hebrew turned up in class with the photograph of one of the manuscripts: it had arrived that morning from Jerusalem and represented chapter 40 of the book of Isaiah. I stared at the picture, slowly deciphered the strange script, and felt in my bones that the document was genuine. At once I became captivated, and after tasting sweet novelty for a few months, I decided with youthful recklessness to devote my life to the study of what was immediately proclaimed 'the greatest ever Hebrew manuscript find of all times'. Against advice, I resolved to write my doctoral dissertation on the Dead Sea Scrolls. Ever since then they and my life have been intertwined.

Ten years of discovery (1947–1956)

The scrolls discovered by the Bedouin Mohammed the Wolf were acquired for peanuts by the Syrian monastery of St Mark in Jerusalem and by Eleazar Sukenik, the Hebrew University's professor of archaeology. On the eve of the outbreak of the first Jewish–Arab war in 1948, the Syrian archbishop, head of St Mark's, smuggled his scrolls to America and advertised them in the *Wall Street Journal*. In due course, an anonymous buyer, secretly representing the new State of Israel, purchased them for $250,000, a quarter of the asking price. Thus all seven scrolls were reunited to be housed in the Shrine of the Book in Jerusalem. Their publication (facsimile edition of the original text with facing transliteration, but without translation or commentary) swiftly followed. American scholars, commissioned by the Syrian monastery, issued in 1950–1 the complete manuscript of Isaiah, and two unknown documents, a Commentary on the Book of Habakkuk and the Community Rule, giving the regulations of an ancient Jewish sect. They were followed in 1954 by Professor Sukenik's posthumous edition of a fragmentary Isaiah Scroll, a collection of Hymns and the Scroll of the War of the Sons of Light against the Sons of Darkness. The most legible part of the poorly preserved seventh scroll, an apocryphal paraphrase of the Book of Genesis written in Aramaic, was published in 1956 by Sukenik's son, Yigael Yadin. By the mid-1950s, literary Dead Sea Scrolls scholarship was successfully launched.

Meanwhile the archaeologists had entered the scene. In 1949 a bored Belgian member of the United Nations Observer Corps persuaded the Jordanian Arab Legion to look for the cave of the Scrolls. They found the hole in the cliff and the French Dominican Roland de Vaux, director of the *École Biblique et Archéologique* of Jerusalem, collected from its floor hundreds of manuscript fragments, some of which belonged to the Scrolls that the Arab shepherd had removed from there two years earlier. Between 1951 and 1956 ten further caves containing five more scrolls and tens of thousands of fragments were discovered mostly by clandestine Arab treasure hunters. The fragments, some large, some small, originally belonged to 900 scrolls, about one quarter of them biblical. They were written mostly on leather, 15% on papyrus, a few on potsherds and one on copper sheets. The texts are chiefly in Hebrew with some Aramaic and a handful of Greek manuscripts. With the help of palaeography, carbon 14 analysis, archaeological data and, when possible, the examination of their content, the texts are dated from the end of the third century BCE to the first century CE.

The work of the archaeologists was not exhausted by the 11 manuscript caves. Having first ignored the nearby ruins, known as Qumran, in the mistaken belief that they were the remains of a fourth century Roman fortlet, Roland de Vaux and his colleagues set out to excavate this ancient settlement as well as a close-by farm further south at Ain Feshkha. The ruins lie within a stone's throw from Cave 4 which yielded nearly two thirds of the Qumran fragments. De Vaux concluded that the main period of occupation of the site fell between the late second century BCE and its destruction by the Romans in 68 CE; that the communal character of the establishment was indicated by a large assembly hall and dining room and over a thousand pots, bowls, plates, etc.; that the adjacent cemetery of some 1200 graves contained mostly male skeletons (but only 5% of the tombs have been examined); and that numerous reservoirs, several furnished with steps, served for ritual purification. The site revealed also a manuscript workshop with inkwells and a potters' installation. Hence de Vaux's surmise that Qumran was a religious settlement and that its occupiers were members of the Jewish sect of the Essenes. The first century CE Jewish writers Philo and Flavius Josephus report their daily purificatory baths, male celibacy and religious communism and their Roman contemporary Pliny the Elder places the Essenes on the western shore of the Dead Sea between Jericho and Engedi. The Essene theory adopted by de Vaux – it was already guessed in 1948 by Eleazar Sukenik and strongly argued by the French scholar A. Dupont-Sommer – quickly gained general acceptance, although during the last 30 years it has been contested, in my opinion largely on questionable grounds.

The latest assault on the Essene origin of the sectarian Dead Sea Scrolls comes from Professor Rachel Elior of the Hebrew University of Jerusalem. Her views, given in interviews, have been loudly trumpeted in the world of the media and may be summed up as claiming (according to the Tel Aviv daily *Haaretz* of 13 March 2009) that the scrolls were written by Jerusalem Sadducee priests and not by Essenes; and that the Essenes never existed, but were invented by the first-century Jewish historian Flavius Josephus.

While a proper assessment of Elior's ideas will have to wait until she backs them with scholarly argument in a forthcoming book in English, the following points need to be made. Josephus was not the first, let alone the only, author to describe (in great detail) the Essenes. He gives two separate accounts of the sect in his *Jewish War* and *Jewish Antiquities* and refers to various Essene individuals involved in Palestinian Jewish history from the mid-second century BCE to the war against Rome in 66–70 CE. Moreover, in his autobiography he states that he himself joined the Essene community for a time. These texts do not look like someone's figment of imagination. Moreover, Josephus was preceded by two other first-century CE writers, the Jew Philo of Alexandria and the Roman Pliny the Elder, both providing a picture of the Essenes essentially the same as that of Josephus, and listing the uncommon features of religious communism and renunciation of marriage. (The Qumran Community Rule also refers to common ownership of property and lays down a way of life unsuitable for married people. Both are contrary to what we know about Sadducee priests.) Finally Pliny the Elder asserts that the Essenes lived on the western shore of the Dead Sea somewhere between Jericho in the north and Engedi and Masada in the south (corresponding to the area where Qumran lies). The two *unique* characteristics (common ownership and male celibacy) and the geographical location remain the solid grounds on which the theory of the Essene identity of the Dead Sea sect continues to stand.

The Scandal Surrounding the Publication of the Qumran Fragments

After the release of the original scrolls between 1950 and 1954, the publication of the fragments from Cave 1 in 1955 promptly inaugurated the collection *Discoveries in the Judaean Desert* (*DJD*)[1] the final volume of which (*DJD*, XL) has just appeared. The snail pace progress of this series during more than three decades up to 1991 constitutes what I once called the academic scandal of the century.

Let me return to 1951. While I was furiously working on my doctorate, I received a visit from one of de Vaux's young Jerusalem collaborators, Dominique Barthélemy, who informed me about the yet unrevealed novelties resulting from the start of the archaeological excavation of Qumran and the discovery by the Bedouin of further scroll caves. On the promise that his identity would be kept secret, he let me use the valuable information he disclosed. So I completed the first ever doctoral thesis on the Dead Sea Scrolls in 1952, which among many other things identified the mid-second century BCE Maccabee brothers, Jonathan and Simon, as the opponents of the Teacher of Righteousness, founder of the Qumran community, a theory that soon became mainstream opinion among scholars. However, before sending my manuscript to the printers, I set sail to Israel to gain first hand experience of the Scrolls.

The great adventure started badly. I was unable to inspect the manuscripts of the Hebrew University: Professor Sukenik was by then gravely ill and died the following year. So I was forced to opt for the riskier alternative which entailed an illegal crossing from Israel to Jordan with false documents. I spent four weeks in Arab Jerusalem at Roland de Vaux's *École Biblique*. At the School I was greeted by my 'secret informant' Barthélemy, and also made friends with the man who was to become the greatest decipherer of Qumran manuscripts, the Pole Joseph Milik. The two young scholars were engaged on editing the fragments discovered in Cave 1. They generously permitted me to study the texts and we shared our ideas about the Scrolls. Whilst there, I also witnessed

Bedouin nervously approaching de Vaux and pulling out from under their *burnous* matchboxes filled with freshly looted scroll fragments which they tried to sell him. Before leaving Jordan, I had the privilege of making my first pilgrimage to Qumran. After only a single season of digging the site was very different from what it looks today. Throughout all my stay Father de Vaux appeared kind and helpful. I was soon to discover his other face.

My book, *Les manuscrits du désert de Juda* (The manuscripts of the Judaean Desert)[2], published at the end of 1953, was warmly acclaimed in the French press. Even *Paris Match*, the Gallic *Hello!* magazine, reviewed it with praise. I was floating in the clouds, but was soon catapulted down to earth by Father de Vaux, the top man in the field. On receiving the copy of the book I sent him and reading in the foreword my thanks to the *École* and himself, he bitterly reproached me with publishing 'friendly' information which was not for release. He even added that simply by mentioning my visit to the *École*, I gave undue authority to my statements some of which were inexact. Totally shattered, I asked him to point out my errors as the second edition of the book was shortly due to appear, but he declined to do so as it would have taken up too much of his time. This reaction of de Vaux gave a foretaste of things to come during the dictatorial tenure of the chief editorship of the Scrolls. Nothing was ethical or correct unless it bore his seal of approval.

When, with the help of the indefatigable Bedouin, ten further caves disgorged their manuscripts, the Barthélemy–Milik cottage industry could no longer cope with the accumulated material. So in 1953/54 de Vaux's brainchild, the 'international and inter-confessional' (though Jew-free) team of editors was created. Its privileged members were to take charge of the fragments, including the colossal heap retrieved in Cave 4. Barthélemy having pulled out, the brilliant Milik became the pillar of the group and seven further, mostly young, researchers were recruited, two from France, two from the USA, two from Britain and one from Germany. There was no supervisory body to oversee the performance of the team. They and de Vaux were a law to themselves. Last, but not least, no proper funding was raised for the continuation of the project. Worst of all, de Vaux set up a 'closed shop': access to the unpublished texts was denied to Hebraists from the outside world until the team had completed their editorial work. This far from satisfactory arrangement did not bode well for the future.

Yet at the beginning the prospects were not gloomy. During the 1950s, the still enthusiastic team assembled, transcribed and largely identified the hundreds of original works and a word concordance was prepared on index cards. Preliminary publications filled the pages of scholarly journals, and by 1962 the contents of the 'minor caves' (2–3, 5–10) appeared in *DJD III*. It comprises insignificant texts with the exception of the Copper Scroll with its list of 64 hiding places crammed with silver and gold. A maverick member of de Vaux's team promptly undertook a treasure hunt, but came back empty handed.

Two factors had a nefarious effect on the editorial project. The lack of finance obliged the members of the team to seek academic appointments away from Jerusalem and turn into part-time or hardly-any-time editors. (Two Harvard University professors practised slow motion editing by proxy, subletting their unpublished texts to clever graduate students.) In June 1967 the Israeli victory in the Six-Day War completely altered the political circumstances. De Vaux and most of the members of the editorial team were pro-Arab, and at the prospect of the Israeli archaeological establishment becoming the chief authority in Scroll matters, de Vaux withdrew to his tent and until his death in 1971 the project remained at a standstill. Only one slim and poor quality volume dealing with the massive Cave 4 material was published during de Vaux's lifetime.

In 1972, the ill-qualified Pierre Benoit, another French Dominican who was not a Hebraist, inherited de Vaux's editorial mantle. Playing the gentlemen, the Israeli archaeological establishment short-sightedly abstained from interfering. I felt it was my turn to step into the breach. By then I held the senior post in Jewish Studies at Oxford and having since 1962 *The Dead Sea Scrolls in English*[3] to my credit, I was in a position to approach Oxford University Press, a body with real muscle as they were the publishers of the Scrolls. The head of the Press, the great Greek papyrologist

C. H. Roberts, was convinced at once and told Benoit to get a move on. The weak chief editor made a semblance of effort, but the French contingent simply did not reply and the three Anglo-Americans politely promised the delivery of the goods between 1974 and 1976, but nothing happened. In despair, I uttered in 1977 my oft-quoted sound bite about 'the academic scandal *par excellence* of the twentieth century'.

Nothing much happened during Father Benoit's reign: only two further Cave 4 volumes trickled in. In 1984 he resigned, and was replaced by John Strugnell, an academically capable Oxford graduate, but a highly inefficient person. Publishing was not his forte. In 1987, on the fortieth anniversary of Qumran, two British colleagues and I tried to breathe fresh life into the moribund editorial process. We organized an international conference in London to which we enticed the editorial team. The aim was to shame them into action. With one exception, they all turned up, made further promises, but my proposal at a public meeting that the photographs of the unpublished documents should be released at once met with blunt refusal from chief editor Strugnell. By then general dissatisfaction with the editorial delays reached boiling point and in the world of the media speculation was rife. Instead of blaming the team, journalists and popular writers dished out a theory of conspiracy: the Vatican decided to prevent the publication of the Scrolls because they contained compromising material for Christianity.

While revolution was brewing, Strugnell was finally demoted on account of an unforgivable *faux pas*. Neither his team mates, nor the Israeli archaeological establishment could stomach his characterization of Judaism, in an interview with a Tel Aviv daily, as a horrible religion which should not exist. Forthwith he was relieved of his office on health grounds: he suffered from manic depression aggravated by alcoholism.

The sensational opening move of the next chief editor, Emanuel Tov of the Hebrew University, chosen by the Israel Antiquities Authority (IAA), was to appoint 6o new members (me included) to the team. But sadly the IAA carried on with de Vaux's 'closed shop': no-one except the selected editors could as much as peep at unpublished texts. This was intolerable, but de Vaux's nefarious policy was already doomed. Its downfall was caused by the IAA and Strugnell.

Following the 1973 Arab–Israeli war, photographic archives of the Scrolls were deposited in 'safe' countries: two in the United States (in Cincinnati and in Claremont, California) and one in the UK (at the Oxford Centre for Hebrew and Jewish Studies). The institutions were obliged to keep the unpublished documents under lock and key. Strugnell in turn published privately for the use of his editorial team 25 copies of a handwritten word concordance of the Qumran texts. Both the photo archives and the concordance leaked.

The concordance came to the hands of a professor in Cincinnati, who with the assistance of a computer-savvy graduate student succeeded in reconstructing from the word list several complete Qumran texts and the Biblical Archaeology Society (BAS) of Washington published them in September 1991. The photo archive given to Claremont was the other source of the leak. All hell broke loose after the unauthorized publication by BAS, and Jerusalem threatened legal proceedings. Meanwhile, in secret, the director of the powerful Huntington Library of Pasadena was getting ready to announce that their photographic collection of the Scrolls would be placed on open shelves. How did they obtain these photos? Mrs Elizabeth Bechtel, a Californian philanthropist and founder of the Claremont Center for Ancient Manuscripts, was given by the IAA two sets of Scroll photos, one for the Center under the usual conditions of inaccessibility, and the other for her private collection of memorabilia. After a quarrel with the trustees of her institute, she donated her own archive to the Huntington with *no restrictive clauses*. A press conference was called in New York on 21 September 1991 to announce the end of the Scroll embargo, but the news transpired in the world of the media. The archaeology correspondent of the London *Times* interviewed me on 19 September and next day, 24 hours before the American press, he scooped the story, quoting my warm approval of the Huntington's action. The IAA soon threw in the towel and after four decades of restrictive practices freedom of inquiry finally triumphed. Hostilities ceased and the images of the manuscripts were made available in photographic, microfiche and CD-ROM form. *DJD* also obtained a new lease of life.

In 1956, Joseph Milik, de Vaux's right hand man, promised a yearly output of two to three *DJD* volumes. De Vaux, Benoit and Strugnell managed a bare eight volumes in 35 years. Tov and his team produced 32 from 1992 to 2009. To mark the completion of the magnum opus, Tov has been awarded the much coveted Israel Prize in Biblical Studies. As for my 250-page *Dead Sea Scrolls in English* of 1962, it became in 2004 *The **Complete** Dead Sea Scrolls in English*, a more than 700-page volume installed among the Penguin Classics.

What have we Learned from Qumran?

To begin with the Hebrew Bible, 200, mostly fragmentary, Qumran manuscripts represent the whole Old Testament except possibly Esther. They agree in substance with the traditional Scripture, the oldest complete Hebrew copy of which dates to 1008 CE. But the Qumran Bible discloses numerous stylistic differences, textual additions or omissions and changes in the order of the passages. The Dead Sea Scrolls prove that the unified traditional text of the Bible was preceded by countless variations and that we owe the definitive form of Scripture to the authoritative intervention of Jewish religious authorities around 100 CE.

In addition to the Bible, a large collection of further religious books circulated among Jews prior to the destruction of Jerusalem in 70 CE. Before Qumran we knew some of these from translation into Greek, Syriac, Ethiopic, etc. The Scrolls have revealed several works in their original form and language, in Hebrew or Aramaic. Previously unknown religious writings have also turned up, considerably enlarging our knowledge of Jewish literature of the age of Jesus. Many of these works, though present among the Dead Sea Scrolls, are thought to have been written by Jews unconnected with the Qumran community. The caves produced also a large number of hitherto unknown compositions, religious rules, poetry, biblical interpretation and a peculiar liturgical calendar, the literary legacy of a sect founded by dissident priests who turned their back on the Temple of Jerusalem. The rule books present an ideal picture of the community next to a practical description. The idealized portrait identifies the group as a miniature Israel. The members believed they lived at the end of time and prepared themselves as sons of light to confront the sons of darkness in a final battle under the leadership of several Messiahs.

On the practical level, the majority of the documents legislate for a community of ordinary Jewish families who followed a stringent regime concerning ritual purity and sexual morality. Members owned property, but were obliged to contribute monthly to a charitable fund. Children born within the community received strict sectarian education and became full members at the age of 20.

The Community Rule, legislating only for male members, substitutes communal existence for family life. Fresh recruits came from the outside Jewish world. They were subjected to an initiation lasting over two years. Their life was characterized by secrecy in regard to the esoteric teachings of the community, by religious communism entailing the obligatory transfer of private property to the sect, and by the adoption of celibacy. The two distinctive characteristics, life out of the common purse and the unmarried state, have persuaded the majority of scholars that the sect was identical with the Essenes, known from first-century CE historians Pliny, Philo and Josephus. Josephus, author of the most detailed account, mentions two Essene branches, one celibate and the other married, echoing the Scrolls.

Qumran has shed fresh light on primitive Christianity, too. Fringe opinion has advanced that Cave 7 housed Greek papyrus fragments of the New Testament, but the weightiest mainstream scholars confute this claim. The parallelism between the Qumran community and Christianity is more subtle. Both the Dead Sea community and the early church considered themselves the true Israel, heirs of the biblical promises. Messianism flourished in both groups, but at Qumran two if not three messianic figures were expected, royal, priestly and prophetic, while in the New Testament as in mainstream Judaism these various figures coalesced into a single person.

In my judgement, the most significant contribution of Qumran to the understanding of the New Testament consists in the expectation of the instant coming of the Kingdom of God in the two communities. Both the Essenes and the early church believed that their respective Masters, the Teacher of Righteousness and Jesus, received from God all the mysteries concerning the final age and passed them on to their followers. They both considered the biblical prophecies fulfilled in the persons and events of their respective communities. Qumran Bible interpretation, especially the fulfilment exegesis, has thrown invaluable light on the Gospels. Both Essenes and Christians eagerly expected in their own days, the former the appearance of the two Messiahs of Aaron and Israel and the latter the reappearance of the triumphant Christ. When they had to admit that their eschatological hopes failed, both attempted to justify the delay, the Essenes through invoking the impenetrable mysteries of God, and the Christians through the comforting idea that the deferred Second Coming provided more time for repentance and was in fact a blessing in disguise.

Notes

1 D. Barthélemy and J. T. Milik, 1955, *Discoveries in the Judaean Desert*, Oxford: OUP.

2 Geza Vermes, 1953, *Les manuscrits du désert de Juda*, Paris: Desclée.

3 Geza Vermes, 1962, *The Dead Sea Scrolls in English*, London: Penguin.

20

The Qumran Community and the Essenes

High among the still debated issues connected with the Dead Sea Scrolls figures the relationship between the Qumran community, attested by the Scrolls and archaeology, and the sect of the Essenes as reported in Greek by two first-century CE Jewish authors, Philo of Alexandria and Flavius Josephus, and in Latin by the Roman geographer and naturalist Pliny the Elder. To simplify the presentation on the Scrolls side, I will concentrate the inquiry on the two principal literary sources describing the Qumran sect, the Damascus Document and the Community Rule. A handy translation of both texts may be found in my *Complete Dead Sea Scrolls in English* published by Penguin in 2004.[1]

The Damascus Document – a Dead Sea Scroll before the Dead Sea Scrolls – was originally revealed by two medieval Cairo manuscripts dating to the tenth and the twelfth centuries, and by 11 fragmentary texts from Qumran Caves 4, 5 and 6. Its second half, the Statutes, describes the structure and discipline of a separatist religious society. It is dated to somewhere close to 100 BCE.

These Statutes legislate for the pre-messianic age, indicated by a passage which speaks of the future coming of two Messiahs, the Messiah of Aaron and the Messiah of Israel. They also hand out moral and ritual rules and define the governance of the 'Damascus' community, a name coined after the phrase 'the New Covenant in the land of Damascus', probably an allegorical designation of Qumran.

The community is envisaged as a miniature biblical Israel, divided into priests, Levites, Israelites and proselytes and is symbolically subdivided into 12 tribes and into camps of thousands, hundreds, and fifties, down to the minimum group of ten.

The 'Damascus' sect was led by priests of the family of Zadok, a clan that supplied the chief priests from the time of Solomon down to the early second century BCE. Even the smallest unit of ten men was to be headed by a priestly Overseer. 'The Overseer of all the camps' was the title of the superior general whose duties included the instruction, examination, rejection or acceptance, ranking and pastoral care of candidates and members. He regulated all the activities of his unit, including business deals, and gave advice in matters of marriage and divorce, too.

Next to the Overseers, the sect had also ten Judges, elected for a specified time. In addition to administering justice, they also handled, together with 'the Overseer', the communal funds maintained by monthly contributions of the members (two days' wages) and destined for the support of the poor. The sectarian judicial system was run on the basis of biblical law adapted to the community's needs.

There were two kinds of new members awaiting initiation: the children of the sectaries who were brought up within the community and adult Jewish outsiders. The former gained full membership at the age of 20. Grown-up Jews were enrolled after one year of study, during which period all the secret teachings of the sect, including its particular solar calendar, were revealed to them.

The 'Damascus' sect consisted of married Jewish couples and their offspring. Among the leaders, explicit reference is made to 'the Fathers' and 'the Mothers', though democratic equality was not part of the system. According to a Cave 4 text, murmuring against 'the Fathers' entailed irrevocable expulsion, but an offender against 'the Mothers' could get away with a penalty of ten days! A husband sleeping with his wife 'against the rules' was declared a fornicator and dismissed from the community. Sectarian matrimony was to be monogamous. Marriage between an uncle and his niece was prohibited and sex between husband and wife was forbidden in Jerusalem (or at least in the area designated as 'the city of the Sanctuary'), no doubt during the three pilgrim festivals of the year.

The Statutes' version of biblical laws concerned with purification and Sabbath observance is generally more rigorous than the practice of the Jews of that age. For instance, on the Sabbath the sectaries were forbidden to assist a domestic animal in labour, nor were they allowed to pull it out from a hole as ordinary Jewish farmers did. Commerce with non-Jews was restricted, but not altogether prohibited.

In short, the 'Damascus' community was a free association of Jewish families, governed by the priests, sons of Zadok, and embracing a more stringent version of the Mosaic law which, together with their sectarian practices, set them apart from the main body of Palestinian Jewry.

The second source, the Community Rule, is also dated to *circa* 100 BCE. Its vantage point is pre-messianic, too, as its community, like the 'Damascus' sect, was still awaiting the arrival of an ultimate prophet and the two Messiahs of Aaron and Israel (1QS 9.11). It has reached us in a complete scroll from Cave 1 and in fragments of 14 manuscripts from Caves 4, 5 and 6.

The Community Rule lays down a stricter set of regulations than the Damascus Document. Its principal peculiarity is the total absence of reference to women. From this is deduced that the members of the group were male celibates. In a mixed-gender association, legislation relating to marriage, female uncleanness, the education of children, and divorce would have been a necessity. Silence here indicates that these matters were not applicable to the community described in this particular rule book.

The Community Rule also envisages a miniature Israel, divided into priests, Levites and laity, and the latter subdivided into 12 tribes, and smaller units down to tens. The representatives of the priestly directorate are designated either as sons of Aaron or, more restrictively, as sons of Zadok.

As in the Damascus Document, the government of the whole congregation and its constitutive parts was in the hands of a priest, called the Overseer, who was assisted by a Bursar. The former presided over the meetings, instructed the members and accepted, rejected and trained new candidates. The Bursar administered the funds and the property of the sect and provided for the needs of the individual members.

The Jewish male volunteers were scrutinized by the Overseer and were made to swear to return to the Law of Moses and observe every single precept of it according to the interpretation of the Sons of Zadok. Any transgression resulted in expulsion.

An indeterminate period of instruction ensued, followed by a public examination. The successful candidates underwent further training during which they were forbidden to touch the pure (solid) food of the community for one year. They had to hand over their property to the Bursar. In the course of the second year of training, the 'novices' could come into contact with the pure food, but were still kept away from the pure drink of the community. After the third examination at the end of the second year, the successful candidates became full members. They were subjected to religious communism, their belongings being turned into communal property.

The new members embraced the community's strict discipline. Apart from celibacy and obedience to superiors, they had to keep away from the irreligious and unclean outside world, Jewish and Gentile. They were also forbidden to communicate the secret teachings of the sect to non-members.

The Rule of the Community contains no precise directives concerning the members' work. All we know is that they had to hand over their salaries to the Bursar, who would spend the money on the community. As for their occupations, the sectaries may have been employed by outsiders and from the archaeological data it may be surmised that at Qumran they practised agriculture and various industries (pottery, tannery) and that some of them were also professional scribes manufacturing books.

The daily routine included at least one communal meal, presided over and blessed by the leading priest. There was also a vigil of prayer, study and discussion occupying four hours of each night. Moreover, the community imagined itself in the pre-messianic age as the spiritual replacement of the Jewish Temple. Qumran was their sanctuary and prayer and holy life were substituted for the sacrifices performed by the priests in Jerusalem.

Considering the problem of identification, how do these pictures of the two varieties of the Qumran community relate to the Jewish separatist religious bodies that existed during the last centuries preceding the destruction of Jerusalem in 70 CE? No doubt a good many small religious parties flourished among the Jews at the turn of the era, but the main groups are the 6000-strong Pharisees, the Sadducees and Zealots–*Sicarii* of unspecified number, and 4000 Essenes, who were joined by the Jewish Christians from 30 CE onwards.

Let us first discard the party of the Sadducees notwithstanding the fact that some of their legal teachings are occasionally echoed in the Scrolls. The lavish life style of the aristocratic Sadducees is irreconcilable with the mode of existence of either of the two branches of the Qumran community. Besides, the Sadducees apparently did not believe in angels or in afterlife of any sort, while the Scrolls are full of angels and are not opposed to the idea of some kind of renewed existence after death.

Similarities with the Pharisees are also noticeable, but only on the general level. They both were devoted to the study and interpretation of Scripture and deeply concerned with legal observance and ritual cleanness. On the other hand, the Qumran community accepted the overall doctrinal supremacy of the priests, whereas Pharisaism was essentially a lay movement, recognizing learning as superior to social class. Furthermore, the Pharisees were outward looking whereas the Qumran sect was closed to the external world, and we cannot find a single record attesting Pharisee insistence on common ownership or property, let alone celibacy.

The Zealots–*Sicarii* theory was first proposed over half a century ago by two Oxford scholars, Professor Sir Godfrey Driver and Dr Cecil Roth. Subsequently it went out of fashion until it was revived by Robert Eisenman in the 1980s. Neither did the laborious attempts to link the Qumran sect with Jewish Christianity make any genuine headway apart from whipping up interest in the popular media.

That leaves us with the Essene hypothesis that has been the front runner ever since Eleazar Lipa Sukenik and André Dupont-Sommer first advanced it 60 years ago. To assess its value, we must set against the archaeological and literary evidence from Qumran the testimony of the classical Greek and Latin sources relating to the mysterious community portrayed by Jewish and Roman first-century CE writers. Philo of Alexandria and Flavius Josephus have left two accounts each and the Roman Pliny the

Elder has produced a brief, splendidly written notice. Noteworthy is the claim of Josephus that at the age of 16 he subjected himself to first hand experience of Essenism.

The etymology and the meaning of the name (*Essaioi* or *Essenoi* in Greek and *Esseni* in Latin) is still debated. Philo derives it from the Greek term, 'the saints' (*hosioi*). Modern scholars tentatively link *Essenes* with a Semitic term, either associated with the Syriac *hase*, 'the pious' or, as I have argued, with the Aramaic '*asen/'asayya* (healers). The latter etymology is supported by Josephus' assertion that the Essenes were experts in the therapeutic qualities of plants and minerals, and devoted themselves to the cure of the sick, and by Philo's description of an Essene-like Egyptian community, called the *Therapeutai* (worshippers-healers), because they healed both the body and the soul.

The Essene congregations dwelt in commonly owned and occupied houses. Members, like the Jewish priests, had to wear white 'sacred' robes. The 'novices' had to undergo instruction for one year before they were admitted to the ablutions of the Essene purity system. A two-year long initiation followed at the end of which an oath of fidelity was sworn and table fellowship granted. Serious breaches of the rules were punished by expulsion as was also the case in the Damascus Document and the Community Rule.

The Essenes practised common ownership of property or, as Pliny puts it, lived 'without money'. Property and earnings were handed over to the superiors and all the needs of the members were catered for by a bursar. Their main occupation was agriculture. Philo asserts that they were forbidden to manufacture weapons. Josephus, on the other hand, concedes that they were allowed to carry weapons for self-protection against robbers. The commonly held idea of Essene pacifism is not borne out by the texts. One of the generals of the Jewish rebels against Rome, John the Essene, was a member of the sect.

Among the Essene characteristics Philo and Josephus list rough appearance (they refused to anoint themselves), frequent ritual baths, the avoidance of spitting and, on the Sabbath, of defecation. The sect rejected marriage according to Philo and Josephus. Pliny bluntly asserts that they lived 'without women, renouncing sex altogether, having only palm trees for company'. The archae-ologists have noted remains of palm trees and a large quantity of date stones at Qumran.

Josephus in an appendix refers to a marrying branch of the sect. Only a regularly menstruating girl, presumed to be fertile, could become an Essene bride. Since sex was permitted exclusively for the propagation of the race, husbands were to keep away from pregnant wives.

The Essenes, declined participation in Temple sacrifices, and symbolically sacrificed among themselves instead. Nevertheless they sent offerings to Jerusalem. They may even have had an es-tablishment in the Holy City somewhere in the area of the 'Essene gate' mentioned by Josephus. Their bread and communal meals were prepared by priests following strict purity rules. They took a purificatory bath before each meal which was preceded and fol-lowed by a grace recited by a priest.

As far as their religious convictions were concerned, the Essenes revered the Law and Moses. They cherished the esoteric doctrines of their own secret books, open only to full members. According to Josephus they were venerated as prophets, able infallibly to foretell the future, and as expert healers.

In the light of the foregoing two canvasses, can one assert that the Qumran community and the Essene sect were one and the same institution? If, to identify the two, absolute accord on every single point is required, the answer must be negative. But bearing in mind the nature of the sources, total unison can hardly be ex-pected. First, the documents are of fundamentally different char-acter. The Dead Sea rules were written by members of an esoteric sect and were intended for the use of initiates only. Conversely, Philo, Pliny and Josephus were outsiders and mostly addressed a non-Jewish readership. Moreover, both Philo and Josephus have produced two descriptions which are not altogether uniform. For these reasons we must allow some elasticity in the evaluation of the sources. After all, even the various Qumran rules indicate different types of organization and occasionally even clash with one another. The variations may be due to diverse causes among which evolving practices are the most likely.

Geographical, chronological and organizational arguments favour the identification of the Qumran community with the Essenes. In particular, Pliny speaks of a famous Essene settlement at a short distance from the western shore of the Dead Sea, where palm trees grew. In a north–south description of the Holy Land the last town he mentions before the Essenes is Jericho and the next two 'below' (*infra*) the Essenes are Engedi and Masada. Qumran would nicely fit this territorial setting if 'below' is interpreted, not as 'lower down', but as 'further south' or 'downstream', on the way to the southernmost site of Masada. The nature of the Qumran ruins (communal buildings, a huge quantity of crockery and many *miqva'ot* – stepped bathing pools – for ritual purification) strongly support the Essene theory.

From the chronological point of view, Qumran was communally occupied at least from 100 BCE to 68 CE. This period suggested by archaeology matches the existence of the Essenes in Judaea as attested by Josephus from Jonathan Maccabaeus (mid-second century BCE) to the great rebellion against Rome (66–70 CE) during which the Essenes had bravely resisted Roman tortures. With the destruction of Qumran, the Essenes disappear from the historical horizon.

The most important proofs of identity are the organizational correspondences. Thus initiation was by stages in both groups. The extremely unusual compulsory common ownership of property characterized the life of the Essenes and of the strictly ascetic Qumran group. The Essenes' renunciation of marriage, except in one of their branches according to Josephus, was equally uncommon. It matches the strict ascetics at Qumran. The Essenes were critical of the Jerusalem Temple and so were the celibate Qumran sectaries. Both considered their community as the place of worship approved by God. The meals, blessed by priests, were reserved only for full members both by the Essenes and by the strictly observant branch that followed the Qumran Community Rule.

However, there are also some differences. The two major discrepancies – common or private ownership and celibate or married form of life – resolve themselves once it is recognized that two separate branches of the same movement are attested both by the Scrolls and by Josephus. Pliny's perfunctory statement that the Essenes lived without money does not tally with the numerous coins found at Qumran, but it may be explained by an artistic liking for a nice turn of phrase. Furthermore, the weighty role of the Zadokite priests, well attested in the scrolls, with their complex liturgical calendar and their messianic expectation, are lacking in the classical sources. But this silence can easily be assigned to the unwillingness of Philo and Josephus to burden their Gentile readers with complicated Jewish theological concepts. Let us further add the total absence in the Scrolls of the term 'Essene', or anything approaching it. Here the most likely reason for the Scrolls' silence is that the sectaries were described as Essenes only by outsiders; the members of the group called themselves 'men of the community', 'men of holiness' or 'men of the Law' in a somewhat similar way as members of the Catholic order of the Franciscans can be commonly designated as 'Grey Friars' and those of the non-conformist Society of Friends are usually called 'Quakers'.

Finally, we may need to adopt a fresh point of view in assessing the relationship between the married and the celibate communities. Josephus gives the impression that the celibate Essenes formed the main group and the marrying branch was an unimportant side shoot. The much more extensive Qumran evidence in favour of the married sect suggests the opposite view, namely that the married sectaries represented the bulk of the movement, but that the fame of the celibate elite of Qumran reached the ends of the earth. 'Unbelievable though this may sound, for thousands of centuries a race has existed which is eternal yet into which no one is born,' Pliny tells us. Understandably, the Jewish apologists, Philo and Josephus were only too glad to propagate this notion and present the Essenes as Jewish religious celebrities to their curious and intellectually hungry Graeco-Roman readers.

Note

1 Geza Vermes, 2004, *The Complete Dead Sea Scrolls in English*, London: Penguin.

21

Midrash in the Dead Sea Scrolls and the New Testament

No doubt a number of speakers addressing this conference on Midrash will discuss the etymology and use of the Hebrew word in question. I may therefore be excused if I jump *in medias res* and take the term *midrash* to mean Bible interpretation.

The purpose of this short paper is to define and illustrate the principal types of Bible interpretation included in the Qumran manuscripts. A great amount of scholarly attention has been devoted to this topic. An excellent recent synopsis is offered by Moshe Bernstein in 'Interpretation of Scripture' in *Encyclopedia of the Dead Sea Scrolls* (2000), pp. 376–82.[1] I myself have published a fair number of articles on the subject, including *Scripture and Tradition in Judaism* (1961),[2] *Postbiblical Jewish Studies* (1975),[3] 'Bible Interpretation at Qumran' in the *Yadin Volume, Eretz Israel 20* (1989), pp. 184–91[4] and 'Biblical Proof-Texts in Qumran Literature' in *JSS 34* (1989),[5] pp. 493–508. Two of my former students have added their contribution to the subject: Jonathan Campbell in *The Use of Scripture in the Damascus Document* (1995)[6] and Timothy Lim in *Holy Scripture in the Qumran Commentaries and the Pauline Letters* (1997).[7]

I intend to sketch Qumran Bible interpretation under six headings:

1 Editorial-type exegesis
2 Harmonizing expansion
3 Explanatory glossing
4 Exegetical supplementation
5 Exegesis of continuous biblical texts
6 Theological exegesis

I propose to end with a cursory glance at the parallel interpretative phenomena in the New Testament.

Editorial-type exegesis

The process thus described is not exactly interpretation but consists in the clarification or alteration of the meaning of a biblical passage through following it up or combining with other extracts from Scripture. Thus Deuteronomy 26.21–3 forbids the planting of an Asherah (a tree) in the Temple courtyard and the setting up of a pillar. Leviticus 26.1 on the other hand prohibits the making of idols, pillars or statues (carved stones) anywhere for the purpose of worship. The 11QTemple Scroll 51.19—52.3 combines all these prohibition in a single law:

> You shall not do in your land as the nations do. Everywhere they sacrifice, plant sacred trees, erect sacred pillars and set up carved stones to bow down before them . . . . You shall not plant [any tree as a sacred tree beside my altar to be made by you.] You shall not erect a sacred pillar [that is hateful to me.] You shall not make anywhere in your land a carved stone to bow down before it.

It is worth noting that the Temple Scroll anticipates Targum Pseudo-Jonathan on the same Leviticus 26.1. There the Targumist aims at justifying the production of mosaic pavements in Jewish synagogues as long as they are purely decorative and are not worshipped.

Harmonizing Expansion

Once more the Temple Scroll unites the precept of Deuteronomy 12.23–4 which obliges a Jew to abstain from the eating of blood – blood is to be spilled on the ground – with Leviticus 17.13 which orders a hunter to cover with dust the blood poured out on the earth. So the Temple Scroll 52.11–2 runs: 'It is the blood alone that you shall not eat. You shall spill it on the ground like water and cover it with dust.'

Explanatory Glossing

A good illustration is furnished by the Commentary on Genesis (4Q252 fr. 1) which appends chronological details to the biblical narrative of the Flood and in doing so adapts the account to the solar calendar of the Qumran community. Genesis 8.3–4 reports that the waters of the flood abated at the end of 150 days and that in the seventh month on the seventeenth day of the month Noah's ark came to rest on the mountains of Ararat. The Qumran commentator, in turn, specifies in conformity with the calendar used by him, that the abatement of the waters lasted two days, namely on the fourth and fifth of the week, and that the ark landed on the mountain on the sixth day of the week, that is, the seventeenth day of the seventh month. The clearest remark indicating that the commentator is guided by the Qumran solar calendar appears at Genesis 8.18 at the beginning of column 2 of the document where a full year of 364 days is mentioned.

Supplementation

The Temple Scroll adjoins a sectarian complement to the Deuteronomic Law regulating the treatment of a captive woman whom a Jewish man proposes to marry. Deuteronomy 21.12–13 advises him to be kind and patient. She must be given a month to readjust herself to her new situation and only then should the man make of her his wife. According to Temple Scroll 63.11–15, after a month of acclimatization the woman may be fit for the bed, but not for the kitchen or the sanctuary. To attain a perfect state of ritual cleanness, she will have to train for a further seven years:

> If you see among the captives a pretty woman and desire her, you may take her to be your wife. You shall bring her to your house, you shall shave her head and cut her nails. You shall discard the clothes of her captivity and she shall dwell in your

house and bewail her father and mother for a full month. Afterwards you may go to her, consummate the marriage with her and she will be your wife. But she shall not touch whatever is pure for you, for seven years, neither shall she eat of the sacrifice of peace-offering until seven years have elapsed.

Note again that Targum Pseudo-Jonathan on Deuteronomy 21.23 obliges the husband of the captive woman to turn his wife into a proselyte.

Exegesis of Continuous Biblical Texts

This important class may be subdivided into two categories: the 'Rewritten Bible' and the '*Pesher*'.

The Rewritten Bible

The 'rewritten Bible', a phrase which to the best of my knowledge I invented in 1961 in *Scripture and Tradition in Judaism* (pp. 67, 95) to describe the midrashic process inserting interpretative developments into the biblical narrative itself, is splendidly exemplified at Qumran by 1Q Genesis Apocryphon. Outside Qumran, the most significant instances are the *Jewish Antiquities* of Josephus, Pseudo-Philo's *Biblical Antiquities* and the various versions of the Palestinian Targums. The Genesis Apocryphon provides many examples of exegetical expansion introduced into elliptic biblical texts without any indication that something has been explicitly added.

In Genesis 12.11–3 Abraham urges Sarah to conceal from the Egyptians the real nature of their relationship and pretend, in order to save Abraham's life, that she is his sister and not his wife. But the Book of Genesis contains no clue as to how Abraham obtained his foreknowledge. The Genesis Apocryphon reveals that he was warned by a dream about a cedar (Abraham) and a palm tree (Sarah). In the dream people came to fell the cedar, but were restrained by the plea of the palm tree. The explanation is fully integrated into the narrative and the reader is not expected to notice that something has been added to the biblical narration. Indeed, we may wonder whether the interpreters were aware of changing the original text when they endeavoured to bring out its full meaning. Interestingly Flavius Josephus expressly asserts that he was faithfully reproducing Scripture without addition or omission (*Ant.* 1.17) when in fact he was doing the extreme opposite. On the other hand, in the Commentary on Genesis (4Q252) the glossator deliberately points out that although it was Ham who behaved disgracefully towards his drunken father, the punishing curse was laid on Ham's son Canaan, because according to Genesis 9.1 God had blessed all the sons of Noah. This same argument survived a long time after Qumran and is handed down in the name of R. Judah ben Ilai in the second century CE.

The Qumran Pesher

The Qumran *pesher* consists in the interpretation of prophetic predictions by indicating their realization in historical personalities or events in the Qumran era. The equation between prophecy and fulfilment remains itself cryptic. A non-initiate is not wiser when he is told that 'the Righteous' is 'the Teacher of Righteousness and 'the Wicked' is 'the Wicked Priest'. However, members of the Community for whom these commentaries were written knew perfectly well who these individuals were. Occasionally equivocation is removed as in the case of the Nahum *pesher* where 'the lion' of the prophet is identified as Demetrius, king of Greece, Demetrius Eucairos, preceded by Antiochus, king of Greece, Antiochus Epiphanes. However, 'the lion's cub', the chief opponent, remains unnamed and is recognizable only by means of the wicked deed attributed to him, namely that he had 'hanged' his adversaries alive, an expression alluding to the crucifixion by the Jewish priest-king Alexander Jannaeus of 800 Pharisees who had been the allies of the Seleucid king Demetrius III.

Examples of a similar type of exegesis have survived in rabbinic literature too. The best known cases are Yohanan ben Zakkai's prediction with the help of Isaiah 10.30 that Vespasian, commander in chief of the Roman forces besieging Jerusalem, would become emperor as he was bound to be the 'Mighty man', that is a king, who would bring down 'Lebanon', that is the symbol of the Temple of Jerusalem. It is worth noting that 4Q285 recognizes in the same 'Mighty man' the 'Branch of David', the 'Prince of the Congregation', i.e. the royal Messiah.

Theological Exegesis

In this class of exegesis a doctrine or moral precept is proved through the appropriate interpretation of one or several Bible quotations. The exegetical process varies from a single proof text to a chain of texts constituting a complex rabbinic midrash-like argument.

Simple exegesis

In the Community Rule the doctrine that preparation for the coming of God's Kingdom must take place in a retreat to the desert is demonstrated through the citation of Isaiah 40.3, 'Prepare in the wilderness the way of **** (the Tetragram), make straight in the desert a path for our God.' The interpreter then continues with the identification of the 'path' as the *midrash* of the Torah commanded by Moses with a view to discovering all the secret instructions handed down by the Prophets.

Complex exegesis

A splendid example of this sort of theological/moral exegesis is yielded by the Damascus Document 4.12—5.13. The author describes the three nets of Belial in which the opponents of the sect were caught. The first of these is the one that concerns us, namely fornication in which the enemies were twice caught. First they were caught when they took a second wife while the first was still alive and they were caught again when they allowed an uncle to marry his niece.

There has been a considerable debate whether the first prohibition is aimed at polygamy only or it includes also remarriage after divorce or, indeed, any second marriage, even the remarriage of a widower. However, the three proof texts, 'Male and female created He them' (Gen 1.27); 'They went into the ark two by two' (Gen. 7.9) and the king 'shall not multiply wives to himself' (Deut. 17.17), clearly show that the author has polygamy in mind. As for the prohibition against an uncle marrying his niece – a practice not uncommon among Jews starting with Abraham who married the daughter of his brother – it is deduced from the parallel interdiction in Leviticus 18.13 of an aunt marrying her nephew with the remark that the reverse is also true for a niece marrying her uncle. In fact the Temple Scroll 66.15 formally enjoins: 'A man shall not marry the daughter of his sister, for this is an abomination.'

To conclude this survey of the classes of Qumran exegesis with an oddity, no doubt meaningful to the readership of the Damascus Document two millennia ago, but striking us today as quasi comical, let us glance at CD 7.14–21. By manipulating the text of Amos 5.26–7, originally meant to convey a divine threat – the Israelites would be exiled beyond Damascus to the much dreaded Assyria – the Qumran author turns it into a promise of salvation. For him Damascus is the land of the New Covenant from where the triumphant Messiah, the Star of Jacob, would arise.

Here ends my bird's eye view of the main varieties of Bible exegesis attested in the Dead Sea Scrolls. I must admit that it was rather optimistic on my part to assume that I could cover so much ground in such short space. A proper treatment of the New Testament must be left for a different forum on another occasion. Speaking in general terms, it should be stated that no book of the New Testament indulges in pure exegesis, the explanation of real or imaginary difficulties in the biblical text. New Testament writers are not interested in commenting on the Hebrew Scriptures for their own sake. Like the authors of the Qumran *pesher*, they are looking in the text of the Bible a message applying to their age and circumstances.

All counted, the New Testament contains about 900 uses of the Bible varying from verbal allusions, i.e. telling a story or formulating a teaching with the help of expressions borrowed from Scripture, to formal *pesher*-type citations and sometimes, especially in Matthew and John, with the explicit claim that the event described came about in order to fulfil the words of a prophet.

St Paul, who received a Pharisee training at the feet of Gamaliel, was able to support his teaching with midrash-type exegesis. In interpretative manoeuvring he was no less skilled than the author of the Damascus Document. Indeed his argument in Galatians 4 demonstrating from Scripture that the Jews were the children of Hagar and the Gentile Christians the children of Sarah would have provoked the secret envy even of the pilpulistic rabbis of Pumbeditha.

Notes

1 Lawrence H. Schiffman and James VanderKam (eds), 2000, *Encyclopedia of the Dead Sea Scrolls*, Oxford: OUP.

2 Geza Vermes, 1961, *Scripture and Tradition in Judaism*, London: Penguin.

3 Geza Vermes, 1975, *Postbiblical Jewish Studies*, Leiden: Brill.

4 Ben-Tor, A, 1989, *Eretz-Israel: Archaeological, Historical and Geographical Studies, 20: Yigael Yadin Memorial Volume*, Jerusalem Israel Exploration Society.

5 Geza Vermes, 'Biblical Proof-Texts in Qumran Liturature' in *Journal of Semitic Studies XXXII:II*, 1989, pp. 493–508.

6 Jonathan G Campbell, 1995, *The Use of Scripture in the Damascus Document*, Walter de Gruyter.

7 Timothy Lim, 1997, *Holy Scripture in the Qumran Commentaries and the Pauline Letters*, Oxford: OUP.

Part Four

Miscellanea

22

The Notion of the Covenant in the Dead Sea Scrolls

More than 50 years ago, against sound advice, I decided to write a doctoral dissertation in a faculty of theology on the historical framework of the then freshly discovered Dead Sea Scrolls (DSS). When the thesis was nearly finished, I was strongly advised by my supervisor to add to my mainly historical research a summary of the doctrinal aspects of the Qumran manuscripts. As I found the existing Old Testament theologies, built on the model of medieval Christian theology, unsuitable for my purpose, I searched for a fundamental Jewish cornerstone and discovered it in the notion of the Covenant or *berit*.

The biblical covenant concept is patterned on that of a pact between a great king and a subject nation. As long as the rules set by the king are obeyed the vassals enjoy royal favour. If not, they pay the consequences of their foolishness.

The Hebrew Bible is the story of successive Covenants between God and the ancestors of Israel and the Jewish people itself. Noah, Abraham: promise of posterity and land against perfect life. Moses: promise of Israel becoming God's elect nation provided they obey the Torah. Joshua: promise of land fulfilled and Israel recommitted itself to God. From then on, disobedience followed disobedience and brought about divine punishment by foreign invaders (Philistines, Assyrians, Babylonians, Greeks, Romans) but by virtue of his promise God spared a small portion of the Jewish people, the faithful Remnant. Saintly leaders, David, Josiah, Ezra inspired repentance and conversion. As time progressed, the idea of Covenant also evolved leading to Jeremiah's 'new Covenant' written in the heart, an idea reformulated in individual terms by Flavius Josephus in the first century CE when he asserted that every Jewish child had the laws of God engraved on his soul.

THE REAL JESUS

Turning to the covenant in the Dead Sea Scrolls, today with the publication in 2004 of the Concordance of the non-biblical DSS, I can statistically justify my youthful choice of covenant as the basic concept of Jewish theology. The word appears in the extant Q texts more than 250 times, the majority of the occurrences being in the three major doctrinal compositions, the Damascus Document (DD), the Community Rule (CR) and the Thanksgiving Psalms from Caves 1 and 4.

The Covenant and occasionally the new Covenant is the foundation on which the Q Community was built. In a time of wickedness (the age of wrath) they repented and became the 'converts of Israel'. They returned to the Torah and the Prophets understood according to the correct explanation received by the Teacher of Righteousness from the mouth of God. This interpretation is expressly defined as 'the last interpretation of the Law'.

Thanks to this God-given exegesis the members of the Q Community were enabled to observe the commandments correctly. The other Jews were thought to err regularly and transgress the Law while they imagined they were adhering to it.

Let me illustrate this with the case of marriage between an uncle and his niece. Mainstream Judaism allowed this because the Bible says nothing about it, Leviticus 18.13 prohibiting only the union between aunt and nephew. We read in the DD:

> Moses said, 'You shall not approach your mother's sister (your aunt); she is your mother's near kin'. But although laws against incest are written for men, they also apply to women. When therefore the brother's daughter uncovers the nakedness of her father's brother, she is also near kin. (CD 5.8–11)

Thus the Qumran teachers claimed that relevant laws applied also to both males and females. Indeed the Temple Scroll expressly declares in a strictly legal style: 'A man shall not take the daughter of his brother or the daughter of his sister.' (TS 66.16–7).

How did one enter the Covenant? Here Qumran introduced a sectarian refinement to the common idea of Judaism. In the Bible every Jew was chosen as a son or daughter of God. By accepting the Torah they all became beneficiaries of the divine covenant, a 'special possession' of God. However, soon a moral distinction crept in. Only the faithful belonged to the covenant; the wicked Israelites excluded themselves from it. 'When the Israelites do the will of God, they are called sons; when they don't, they are not called sons' (Palestinian Talmud, Kiddushin 61c).

The innovation produced by Qumran individualized the concept of election. People became members of the Community of the Covenant, not automatically as a baby by birthright, but through the personal commitment of an adult. For this they had to wait until they had reached the age of 20. Even the children of married sectaries who had been brought up in the Community had to undergo a solemn initiation.

This allusion to married sectaries necessitates an explanation. The Scrolls reveal that there were two branches of the Community. One, described in the Damascus Document, consisted of ordinary Jewish families – father, mother and children – who were distinguished from mainstream Jews by their life style defined by the *halakhah* or legal customs of the sect. But they owned property and kept their earnings. Nevertheless they were obliged to contribute monthly to a charitable fund administered by the leaders and judges of the sect. In my view, these married sectaries formed the majority as against the branch of an elite minority which adopted a much more ascetic existence. They were subjected to a lengthy period of initiation (2–3 years), were bound by strict obedience to their elders and betters, adopted religious communism and, it would seem, celibacy. It is true, celibacy is nowhere expressly stated in the Scrolls, but the CR, unlike the DD, while giving a detailed description of their mode of living, nowhere mentions marriage, divorce, children, education, etc. Women simply play no part in the sectarian existence envisaged in the CR.

At this point two comments are apposite:

1 The Community, as emerging from the Scrolls, resembles or is identical with the sect of the Essenes described by the ancient Jewish writers, Philo of Alexandria (c. 20 BCE – c. 40 CE) and

Flavius Josephus (37 CE – c. 100 CE) and the Roman Pliny the Elder who died in 79 CE in the eruption of Vesuvius. They record that the Essenes lived in an organized community, owning everything in common and rejecting marriage. However, Josephus notes that some of the Essenes were married. Thus Josephus can be quoted in support of both branches of the Dead Sea sect, the married and the celibate.

2 The Qumran settlement as revealed by archaeology points to a religious community rather than to private occupation. The connection of the site with the Scrolls is hardly questionable. Cave 4, the place where the bulk of the manuscript fragments were found, lies within a stone's throw from the buildings. The buildings themselves, with their large rooms and their industrial quarter suggest a community rather than individual families. Considerable quantities of plates, bowls, pots and pans were discovered. The pottery was baked in an oven on the site and a tanner's workshop no doubt produced the leather required for the production of scrolls. Several inkwells have also survived. Numerous pools were used for ritual bathing.

Q appears to be the centre of a religious movement probably identical with the place described by Pliny as situated on the western shore of the Dead Sea between Jericho and Engada. It was there that the Essenes dwelt 'without women, renouncing sex entirely, without money, having for company only the palm trees' (Natural History 5.17.4).

The evidence supplied by the CR and the archaeological ruins of Qumran, combined with the testimony of Pliny, present a strong argument in favour of an identification of the *Yahad*, the Community whose members were known as the men of the Covenant, with a group of male celibates, and ultimately with the Essenes of Philo, Josephus and Pliny. On the other hand, archaeology confronts us with a counter-argument: some women and children were also buried in the Qumran cemetery.

The evidence is complex. Bear in mind the relatively small number of the graves which have been examined (43 out of

c. 1200). When I asked a renowned Israeli archaeologist during the golden jubilee conference of Qumran in 1997 whether there was any chance of investigating more tombs, I was told that owing to the influence of ultra-religious Jews opposed to the opening of graves, this could happen only if Qumran came under Palestinian or Jordanian administration. Of course, the work could have been done before the Six-Day War of 1967, but it was not performed; I was told by the man who did the partial survey of the graves (Henri de Contenson) that opening graves which contained only bones and no jewels or artefacts was so boring that they just could not be bothered. We are also told that some of the female and child remains may represent modern Bedouin burials.

Be this as it may, while the skeletons of women and children were mostly found in peripheral graves, there were at least two women in the main part of the cemetery. But even if all of them are counted, their number is quite disproportionate to that of the male skeletons. They do not correspond to a cemetery of ordinary married people where owing to high infant mortality one would expect to find a considerable amount of remains of young children. This is a puzzle which I will endeavour to deal with at the end of this talk.

Returning to my main topic, the CR includes a highly significant section for the understanding of what membership of the sect of the Covenant meant for the Qumran insiders. In its longer version the CR from Cave 1 starts with a religious ceremony, the liturgy of the entry into the Covenant. (This section is missing from at least one of the Cave 4 versions and may represent a later addition to the core part of the CR). In this ceremony, the newly qualified members who had completed their long initial training vowed that they would turn away from their former infidelities and obey every single precept of the Law of Moses according to its correct interpretation by the priestly teachers of the sect. Ritual immersion (a full baptism) followed, but it was specified that real purification would not ensue unless the symbolic ritual cleansing was accompanied by the conversion of the heart.

Together with the new initiates the existing members also renewed their allegiance to the Covenant of the Community. Before the ceremony the moral progress, or the lack of it, was considered and recorded by the leaders in the case of each sectary and the members were renumbered according to their spiritual seniority. This ranking had a practical importance because in their meetings no junior was allowed to speak before his seniors or was allowed to interrupt their speech. For downgrading a member, the superior could rely on a register in which the reported misbehaviour of a culprit was recorded.

Curiously, a small and unfortunately badly damaged fragment found in Cave 4 (4Q477) lists the names of such transgressors and their failings: Yohanan was short-tempered; Hananiah Notos disturbed the community spirit; a member whose name has disappeared was guilty of favouring his relatives; Hananiah son of Simon loved something prohibited (the sin has disappeared in the gap). It is typical and pathetic that the only surviving real names of members of the Community are those of the naughty boys. (Unless the contested opinion of F. M. Cross and Esther Eshel is accepted which sees in an *ostrakon* (an inscribed potsherd) discovered on the Qumran site a draft deed of gift in which a new member of the *Yahad*, Honi handed over his slave Hisdai to Eleazar son of Nahmani, apparently the bursar of the Community.)

The ceremony of the Entry of the Covenant seems to have brought together all the members of the Community whether they belonged to the celibate or to the married branch – the DD refers to the annual assembly of all the camps. From a Cave 4 fragment of the DD we learn that the Feast of the Renewal of the Covenant took place in the third month. This was no doubt the Feast of Weeks (*Shabuot* or Pentecost), the commemorative festival of the gift of the Torah by God to Moses on Mount Sinai.

Pious participation in this solemnity was believed to bring about spiritual transformation and renewal. I will quote from CR:

> He (the member of the Community) shall be cleansed from all his sins by the spirit of holiness uniting him to His (God's) truth, and his iniquity shall be expiated by the spirit of uprightness and humility. And when his flesh is sprinkled with purifying water and sanctified by cleansing water, it shall be made

clean by the humble submission of his soul to all the precepts of God. Let him then order his steps to walk perfectly in all the ways commanded by God concerning all the times appointed for him, straying neither to the right nor to the left and transgressing none of His words, and he shall be accepted by virtue of a pleasing atonement before God and it shall be to him a Covenant of the everlasting Community. (1QS 3.6–12)

This yearly get-together of all the members of the sect, a kind of annual pilgrimage to the centre at Qumran, may also provide a solution to the dilemma created by the cemetery lying just outside the Dead Sea settlement. If the Feast of the Renewal of the Covenant took place at Qumran and was attended not only by the celibate sectaries, but also by their married brethren accompanied by their wives and children, some of them may have died during their pilgrimage. This may therefore account for the presence of a small number of women and children buried in the predominantly male graveyard of Qumran overlooking the Dead Sea.

23

Tax-Collectors

Tax-collectors have had a bad press throughout the ages. Like their modern successors people in antiquity considered them as interfering busybodies who tried to deprive the citizen of his hard-earned money. They were generally believed to be rapacious, always imposing charges much heavier than was appropriate.

In Old Testament times, during the existence of the Judaean and the Israelite kingdoms, dues to the monarch were paid either in the form of unpaid labour or in kind. Jars originally filled with wine, oil or grain carry the inscription: 'To the king'. It was only with the arrival of the Persian kings as rulers of Judaea, between the sixth and fourth century BCE, that the Jewish lay population was required to contribute monetary 'tribute, custom or toll' to the Persian royal treasury (Ezra 4.13). It is interesting to note that the priests and Levites were tax exempt (Ezra 7.24)! Still in Persian times, under the governorship of Nehemiah, the Jewish male population was obliged to make a single payment of one third of a shekel of silver per person for the maintenance of the Temple of Jerusalem (Neh. 10.32–3), a rule subsequently changed to an annual contribution of half a shekel as Temple tax. It was still valid in New Testament times: the curious story of St Peter catching a fish with a shekel coin in its mouth provides miraculous means for Jesus and Peter to pay their dues without using their own money (Matt. 17.24). After the destruction of the Jerusalem sanctuary in 70 CE the Flavian emperors continued to collect the same tax, renamed as the Jewish tax (*fiscus Iudaicus*), and used it for the support of the temple of Jupiter Capitolinus in Rome. It was abolished by the Emperor Nerva in 96 CE.

The first reference to tax-collectors belongs to the period when Palestine was under Egyptian Greek (Ptolemaic) domination after the conquest of the Near East by Alexander the Great (356–23 BCE). An eminent Jewish family, known as the sons of Tobias, flourished at the turn of the third and second centuries BCE. Its most prosperous member was Joseph, who married the sister of the Jewish High Priest, and obtained for 22 years from the Ptolemaic rulers the lease of taxes of Syria, Phoenicia, Judaea and Samaria. This meant that he undertook to deliver to the king a fixed sum, but was free to collect as much as he could from the citizens of the provinces. The glorious fortress built at Araq el-Emir in Transjordan testifies to the great prosperity enjoyed by the family.

There are numerous references to tax-collectors or publicans in the first three Gospels. To understand their role in the first century CE, we must glance at the financial administration of the Jewish territory from the Roman conquest of Palestine by Pompey in 63 BCE to the age of Jesus. Under both Roman and Herodian government moneys collected from citizens belonged to two categories. Direct taxes were paid on landed property and there was also a poll tax imposed on each individual. There were in addition duties, tolls or customs levied on transported goods. The two kinds of tax were collected by different means and by different officials.

When Pompey turned Judaea into a Roman province in 63 BCE, the taxes set by him, 60 million shekels, were first to be gathered by the Jewish High Priest, but in 57 BCE he was relieved of this duty and the country was divided into five districts, based on five major cities, for the levying of the tributes through tax-farmers. Julius Caesar changed the system in 44 BCE and appointed Antipater, the father of Herod the Great, as procurator or tax plenipotentiary of Judaea.

Herod the Great (37–4 BCE) gained exemption from paying taxes to Rome in 30 BCE when he was recognized as a client king by the Emperor Augustus. He collected, however, his own taxes from the Jewish people probably with the help of tax-farmers. When after the dismissal of Archelaus, son of Herod, as ethnarch of Judaea in 6 CE, Quirinius, governor of Syria, conducted a census with a view to reorganizing the Judaean taxation system for the Romans by preparing a record of the population and of the landed property. (This census was antedated by St Luke to coincide with the birth of Jesus at the end of the reign of Herod.) The monies, except the sums which were siphoned off by corrupt officials, ended up in the imperial treasury as the Gospel episode of the dispute about paying tax to Rome illustrates: 'Whose likeness and inscription is this? They said, Caesar's. Then he said to them, "Render to Caesar the things that are Caesar's"' (Matt. 22.20–1). In Galilee, Antipas, the other son of Herod, remained free during the life of Jesus to levy tributes for himself and not for the Romans. The apostle Matthew, a former publican, was in his employ. Shortly before the outbreak of the great rebellion of the Jews against Rome in 66 CE we learn that the leading members of the Sanhedrin (the chief priests, aristocrats and legal experts) set out to raise the taxes from the discontent population, unsuccessfully trying to avoid the conflict with Rome.

Whether they admitted it or not, the ordinary people benefited from the taxes. Herod's construction of the port of Caesarea and the road network created by the Roman armies greatly improved international commerce. Likewise the many aqueducts built in the cities were a blessing for the population. The Herodian architectural improvements in Jerusalem, including the renovation of the Temple, made the city more attractive to visitors and encouraged pilgrimage, the religious tourism of the age. The presence of the Roman legionaries and the well-functioning judicial system guaranteed reasonable public peace and security. These are the positive values deriving from taxation.

In addition to urban tax offices, there were also in Galilee and in Judaea customs posts on the main trade routes. These were manned by entrepreneur publicans who undertook to pay an agreed sum to the local authorities and saw to it that enough money was obtained from the travelling merchants to secure for them a good living after they had paid their dues to the city councils. We know that there were custom posts at Gaza, controlling the approach from Arabia and Egypt, Ascalon, Jaffa, Caesarea and Jerusalem. The Gospels mention two Jewish publicans: Matthew or Levi, who alone was in charge of the customs office, possibly just a table by the main road, in Capernaum leading to the Golan and beyond (Matt. 9.9; Mark 2.14), and Zacchaeus, who was chief publican (*architelones* in Greek), who was the wealthy boss of a company of customs officers in Jericho (Luke 19.1).

In rabbinic literature the tax-collectors have a very bad reputation. They were suspected of ritual impurity for handling unclean goods and for avoiding levying the tithe on their share of the receipts. They were all presumed to be robbers and extortioners. The view found in the Gospels is similar to that of the rabbis. John the Baptist exhorts the publicans not to collect more than the right amount and the repentant Zacchaeus proposes to recompense fourfold everyone he has defrauded. Theirs was a risky business and the extra sum collected from those who were willing to pay covered the loss caused by tax evaders and replenished the pockets of the publicans.

The Talmud, on the other hand, occasionally testifies to the spirit of generosity which Christians associate with Jesus. In the rabbinic version of the parable of the Royal Wedding Feast where, as in the Gospel, the invited guests all fail to turn up, the host on this occasion is a publican by the name of Bar Ma'yan. He invites all the notables of the city to a dinner but they all let him down. So Bar Ma'yan fills the dining hall with the poor of the neighbourhood and feasts with them. When he dies this one good deed of his annuls all the cheatings and robberies of a lifetime (Jerusalem Talmud Sanhedrin 23c) and he is allowed into Paradise.

In the New Testament the publicans play a dual role, one contradicting the other. They on the one hand typify the wicked ('For if you love those who love you, what reward have you? Do not even the tax-collectors do the same?', Matt. 5.46) and are considered as bad as the Gentiles ('If he refuses to listen even to the church, let him be to you as a Gentile and a tax-collector', Matt. 18.17). But on the other hand they are presented as the model of repentance. The apostle Matthew is said to have been a penitent tax-collector who entertained Jesus in the company of his colleagues, 'publicans and sinners' (Mark 2.15). Indeed Jesus was mocked by his critics as the friend of such dishonourable people (Matt. 11.19). Just as John the Baptist's best converts were 'the tax-collectors and the harlots' (Matt. 21.32), Jesus also chose the publicans and the prostitutes as the best subjects of his redemptive mission: 'I came not to call the righteous but sinners' (Mark 2.17).

24

Christian Origins in a Nutshell

With the so-called Edict of Milan, in which the Roman emperor Constantine, following his victory in 312 CE over his rival Maxentius, granted imperial favour to the previously persecuted Christian Church, Christianity became a publicly recognized religio-social reality in 313 CE. In 325 CE the same Constantine summoned and opened the ecumenical council of Nicaea, at which 318 bishops, mostly representing the Greek Church, declared Jesus God, consubstantial with the Father. According to the Nicene Creed, the essential beliefs of Christianity entailed the Holy Trinity – Father, Son and Holy Spirit – the Incarnation of the Son, the redemption of mankind through the crucifixion and resurrection of Christ, and the universality of the Church established to guide and nourish the faithful until the final judgement and the inauguration of eternal life.

From then on the influence of Christianity on public life, exercised under the direction of bishops, ascetics and theologians, steadily increased in the Roman Empire. At Nicaea, the heresy of Arius, who denied the true divinity of Jesus, was refuted by St Athanasius of Alexandria. During the fourth century, the theology of the Holy Trinity was fully developed by the Greek Church Fathers, St Basil, St Gregory of Nyssa and St Gregory of Nazianzus. In the West, St Ambrose and especially St Augustine were the shining lights over the whole spectrum of theological doctrine. Origen of Alexandria in the East and St Jerome in the West dominated the field of biblical studies, and the Egyptian Desert Fathers, led by St Anthony, sowed the seeds of Christian asceticism. Monastic life was finally organized by St Benedict in the sixth century and his disciples were largely responsible for the transmission of classical civilization to western Europe. After the fall of Rome in 476 CE, the Papacy, especially with Gregory the Great (590–604 CE), took on a significant role in the religious, cultural and political life, and Christianity played a leading part in the history of the Middle Ages.

Though fundamentally Hellenistic in thought from the second century onwards, and Roman in organization after Constantine, the Christian movement was originally the product of the Jewish mind. Fully developed Christianity did not fall from heaven. Its beginnings and early progress may be detected and followed in the writings of the New Testament (c. 50–120 CE).

The New Testament consists of 27 Greek documents, four Gospels or theological lives of Jesus, the Acts of the Apostles, outlining the early history of the Christian Church, 21 letters discussing Christian belief and practice addressed to named or anonymous Churches or Church leaders, and the apocalyptic Book of Revelation describing the ultimate victory of Christ and God, marked by the descent on earth of the heavenly Jerusalem. Of these the Fourth Gospel (of John) and the letters of St Paul provide the best insight into the evolution of Christian theology, while the Gospels of Mark, Matthew and Luke and the Acts of the Apostles constitute the chief sources for the understanding of Christian origins.

The author of the Fourth Gospel, imbued in Hellenistic mysticism and philosophy, can hardly be identical with the apostle John, the 'uneducated and common' Galilean fisherman of Acts 4.13. His Jesus, a stranger from heaven, presented as the temporal incarnation of the eternal Word of God, is the first major step towards the deification of Christ in the Nicene Creed. This Gospel probably originated between 100 and 110 CE. It was compiled before 125–150 CE (the date of the earliest papyrus fragments of John), but after the completion, in the final quarter of the first century, of the doctrinally much less developed Synoptic Gospels.

The next chief artisan of Christianity was St Paul, a Jew of the Greek Diaspora (from Tarsus in Asiatic Turkey). He had not known the historical Jesus, and built his doctrine partly on tradition and partly on mystical vision and insight. In his letters to churches founded by him through Syria, Asia Minor, Greece and

Rome, he depicted Jesus as the Redeemer of Jews and Gentiles thanks to his death and resurrection and proclaimed his impending return to earth to bring about salvation for the whole of mankind. Paul's theological vision of the work of Christ was recorded in Greek in his genuine epistles (Romans, 1 and 2 Corinthians, Galatians, Philippians, Philemon, 1 and 2 Thessalonians) approximately between 50 and 60 CE, testifying to a beginning Christological speculation half a century before the Fourth Gospel.

The earliest stage of the tradition relative to the historical Jesus is preserved in the Gospels of Matthew, Mark and Luke. They are called the Synoptic Gospels, because they follow the same general point of view and story line, and can be set out in three parallel columns in a Gospel synopsis. They represent the least evolved form of the portrait of Jesus and are commonly dated to 70–100 CE.

The entire New Testament, including the Synoptic Gospels, is in Greek and was probably composed in Greek. However, Jesus and his original audience were Aramaic-speaking Galilean Jews. It is possible that among early Jewish-Christian groups, such as the Ebionites or the Poor, there existed an Aramaic Gospel. Church tradition refers to Matthew recording the teaching of Jesus in the Hebrew dialect, but no traces of it have survived. In fact, apart from a few Aramaic phrases preserved in Mark's Gospel (e.g. *Abba* = Father, *Talitha cum* = Little girl, rise), Jesus' own words have all faded from memory. The fact that the New Testament was handed down in Greek played an essential part in the transformation of the original Semitic Gospel into a Hellenistic religious system created by philosophically educated Greek Church Fathers.

The Synoptic Gospels, of which Mark is thought to be the earliest (composed c. 70 CE, followed by Matthew and Luke between 80–100 CE), offer a theologically less developed life story of Jesus of Nazareth (c. 6/5 BCE –30 CE), a Galilean charismatic healer, exorcist and teacher, who preached a message of repentance and invited his followers to prepare themselves for entry into the Kingdom of God. His mission was cut short by the intervention of the Roman governor Pilate who, on charges levelled against

Jesus by the Jewish priestly authorities, condemned him to die on the cross. His disciples claimed, however, to have seen him alive in repeated visions and were convinced that the success of their charismatic healing and teaching activity in the name of Jesus was the proof that God had raised him from the dead.

25

The Great *Da Vinci Code* Distraction

In the beginning, before the recent media frenzy about a dastardly conspiracy over Christian origins, there was Dan Brown who, after writing several detective stories, begot *The Da Vinci Code* (2003).[1]

He penetrated the dark central mystery and disclosed that the marriage of Jesus to Mary Magdalene had been hushed up for two millennia by a clandestine clique within the Church. The book was fruitful and multiplied. It became a big hit in 70 languages of the creation, procuring Brown royalties from the sale of 40 million copies.

In Chapter 2, Michael Baigent and Richard Leigh, authors of the 1982 bestseller *The Holy Blood and the Holy Grail*,[2] begot *The Da Vinci Code* court case. They accused Brown of plagiarism: *The Holy Blood and the Holy Grail* had already told the world that Jesus and Mary Magdalene were Mr and Mrs Christ.

Then a sensible judge rejected their claim and landed them with a six-figure legal bill. But the idea that Jesus married the Magdalene woman was not new. It was foreshadowed by Nikos Kazantzakis's novel *The Last Temptation of Christ*,[3] filmed by Martin Scorsese.

An even more picturesque story can be found in Barbara Thiering's *Jesus the Man* (1992),[4] a wholly idiosyncratic interpretation of the Dead Sea Scrolls and the New Testament in which Jesus fathers two sons and a daughter by Mary Magdalene before divorcing her and finding solace with Lydia, a woman bishop with whom he has another daughter. But in fact there is not a single ancient source for the invention of a sexual relation, marital or extramarital, between Jesus and Mary of Magdala.

Chapter 3 revolves around *The Gospel of Judas*, recently published in an edition by Rodolphe Kasser and others.[5] In this not very significant late-second century text, Judas does not betray Jesus but obeys his orders to hand him over to the chief priests.

On Palm Sunday, this 'Gospel', originally begotten by an Egyptian Gnostic sect, was turned, with the help of a two-hour programme on the National Geographic television channel, into a rewritten New Testament that could be watched on five continents. The media furore was of almost nuclear proportions. The internet is still buzzing. The Pope, the Archbishop of Canterbury and the Patriarch of Moscow preached against this new peril to the faith.

Finally, up steps the loser in the *Da Vinci Code* case; Michael Baigent, having freshly begotten *The Jesus Papers*.[6] His latest attempt to put the record straight about the New Testament arrives in time for the wave of publicity building up for the release of the film of *The Da Vinci Code*.

Baigent's story is familiar in presenting Jesus and Mary Magdalene as husband and wife. What is new is the claim that Jesus did not die on the cross. With the connivance of Pontius Pilate, he was taken down alive, nursed back to health and, in the company of Mary Magdalene, lived happily, if not ever after, at least until the middle of the first century.

How serious a threat are these 'revelations' to the picture of Jesus? *The Da Vinci Code* is a category apart. It is fiction and does not pretend to rewrite history. As a novelist, Brown is free to write whatever he chooses. The phenomenal success of the book and, no doubt, of the movie, does not claim to be anything other than fiction, even if it does not derive wholly from originality or from literary genius. No one would mistake Brown for the new Graham Greene. A good conspiracy yarn is highly attractive, but there is more to it, as I will suggest later.

In *The Jesus Papers*, Baigent offers a revisionist theory, shown in his subtitle, *Exposing the Greatest Cover-Up in History*. In his view, Jesus survived Good Friday and enjoyed 15 or 20 years of marital bliss in Egypt. This assertion is counter to the one aspect of New Testament history on which all ancient sources and modern historians agree. For whatever one may think about the birth, miracles or resurrection of Christ, one can be sure that he truly died crucified.

But Baigent's ideas about the cross are no more original than those about Mary Magdalene. It is a rehash of *The Passover Plot*,[7] Hugh Schonfield's 40-year-old flight of fancy about a fake crucifixion. Incidentally, the Koran has also been interpreted as discarding the idea that Jesus died on the cross. According to the Ahmadiyya sect of Islam, he left the Holy Land and emigrated to India, ending his life in Kashmir.

Baigent's account is wrapped in mystery. The silliest aspect of it is the title, hinting at previously unknown 'Jesus papers'. Having teased his readers with this idea, he comes to the top-secret denouement. In the 1960s, an Israeli friend of Baigent, a wealthy antique dealer who wanted to remain anonymous, laid his hands on two long Aramaic letters on papyrus, apparently dated to 34 CE. The friend said that he had consulted the greatest Israeli archaeologists of the time, Yigael Yadin and Nahman Avigad, who had declared the texts 'genuine and important'.

The plot thickens. Yadin and Avigad were indiscreet and news of the discovery reached Pope John XXIII who, the friend alleged, personally instructed the Israeli experts to destroy the documents. They dutifully passed on the papal edict and, to pacify the Pope, the owner of the letters agreed to delay publishing them for 25 years.

After much secret toing and fro-ing, Baigent was finally shown the two papyri. But here comes the anticlimax. Our author, 'a religious historian and leading expert in the field of arcane knowledge', turns out to be a self-confessed ignoramus in ancient languages. Baigent held in his hands the texts of his dreams, but could not read them.

So we are presented with the nameless owner's unsubstantiated assertion that the letters were written to the Jewish High Court by Jesus. He calls himself, according to Baigent's informant, 'the Messiah of the Children of Israel' or *bani meshiha* – the phrase is gibberish. This Jesus reassures the Jerusalem Sanhedrin that he is not God. Some evidence – especially as the Yadin and John XXIII story is unprovable and the letters seem to have vanished without trace.

The Da Vinci Code is a novel, *The Jesus Papers*, to put it mildly, is 'imaginative' remodelling of history. But *The Gospel of Judas* is neither fiction, nor faction, but an ancient document dating to the second half of the second century CE.

It is a typical product of Greek (Platonic)-Christian speculation. Gnosticism flourished among pagans, Jews and Christians. For Gnostics, only the spirit was good. Matter, such as the body, was evil as it derived from the inferior creator, or demiurge, identified by the Christian branch of the Gnostics with the deity of the Old Testament – the maker of Heaven and Earth. The Supreme Being, represented by Jesus and, according to the Gnostics, worshipped by Judas, brings salvation not through the sacrifice of Christ – as it would have involved his flesh – but through mystical enlighten-ment (*gnosis*). Judas helped this process of redemption by assist-ing the Jewish authorities' arrest of Jesus and bringing about his liberation from the prison of his body.

Seen through the warped Gnostic perspective, the murderer Cain, the depraved people of Sodom and Gomorrah, and above all Judas were the true righteous, while the 11 other apostles and the holy men of the Old Testament were ministers of error. Once this is understood, it becomes obvious that a second-century Hellenistic-Gnostic picture of Judas contributes nothing to the understanding of the early first-century Jewish reality in which Jesus and Judas lived. Hence *The Gospel of Judas* supplements our knowledge of Gnosticism, but is irrelevant to our study of the life of Jesus.

So how could a not particularly outstanding detective fiction, a questionable 'investigative' history or a second-rate eighteen-century-old Coptic philosophico-theological speculation become media sensations in our sophisticated twenty-first century? The phenomenon is not new. Since large parts of the population of the Western world ceased being under the direct influence of tra-ditional religion, more and more people have wondered whether there was something not wholly satisfactory in the time-honoured and often fossilized explanation of the origins of Christianity handed down by the churches. Scholars share this sentiment, as witnessed by 200 years of questing for the historical Jesus.

It is no surprise then that, since the nineteenth century, each new archaeological discovery – real, or more recently, thanks to the media, fictional – has been greeted by the public as a long-awaited key to the mystery. The Mesopotamian clay tablets about the dying and rising god, the mystery of the redeeming Persian god Mithra, the Oriental and Hellenistic salvation mysticism of the Roman Empire in New Testament times, and in the mid-twentieth century the Dead Sea Scrolls, were acclaimed as the longed-for clue to the truth.

The archaeological finds have all taught us something new, but the best source for reconstructing the portrait of the historical Jesus has been available all the time. It lies in the New Testament – provided it is interpreted with a view to discovering what the original writers meant to convey to the original readers.

This genuine message about a Galilean faith-healer and preacher of the coming Kingdom of God was progressively concealed under the successive garbs of the mystical vision of St Paul and the Fourth Gospel, and the Greek philosophical imagery of the early church fathers and centuries of accretion inspired by the doctrinal and practical – often political – needs of later Christianity.

Today, theologians and secular historians of religion, working hand in hand and using the latest linguistic, archaeological and cultural tools, should be able to retrieve the authentic Gospel of Jesus, his first-hand message to his original followers. The high dignitaries of the churches would do better to encourage and applaud them than to focus their ire on trivia.

Notes

1 Dan Brown, 2003, *The Da Vinci Code*, London: Corgi.

2 Michael Baigent, Richard Leigh and Henry Lincoln, 1996, *The Holy Blood and the Holy Grail*, London: Arrow Books.

3 Nikos Kazantzakis, 1960, *The Last Temptation of Christ*, London: Faber & Faber.

4 Barbara Thiering, 1992, *Jesus the Man*, New York: Simon & Schuster.

5 Rodolphe Kasser, 2006, *The Gospel of Judas*, London: National Geographic Society.

6 Michael Baigent, 2006, *The Jesus Papers*, New York: HarperCollins.

7 Hugh Schonfield, 2005 (40th anniversary edition), *The Passover Plot*, New York: Disinformation Company.

26

What's Sex Got to Do with It?

Hardly a day passes without my encountering articles or programmes with glaring headlines in which religious leaders of every denomination proclaim what is for them the certain truth. And, confirming what I was told by a friend of mine – 'Christians are all as hung up on sex as Jews are on food' – the certain truth is usually of a sexual nature.

Recent subjects have included the fallibility of the condom as protection against the HIV virus; the immorality of contraception; the identification of abortion with murder; the refusal to extend sex equality to women and ordain them priests and bishops, and the harsh treatment of homosexuals, even celibate ones.

Christianity has not always been a religion so preoccupied with sexual behaviour (or gender identity). Theology used to challenge ideas; people's behaviour in bed did not rank among its top concerns.

Consider the arguments which raged at the time of the Reformation. The reformers and counter-reformers aimed much higher than their latter-day heirs and focused on the ultimate source or sources of the Christian faith. Was it scripture alone or scripture and tradition or ultimately the Magisterium, the Christ-given doctrinal authority of the church?

Yet even these issues appear prosaic compared with the subtle polemics which characterized Christianity in the early centuries of its existence. It will surprise contemporary pedestrian pragmatics that the first conflict in the church was provoked not by the claim, based on the fourth Gospel (dating to the early second century CE) regarding the divinity of Christ, but by the reality of his humanity.

These dissident Christians, called Docetists, held the suffering and death of Jesus to be purely imaginary. Two hundred years later the burning issue was a highly speculative, metaphysical teaching of an Alexandrian cleric named Arius about the son of God, who, according to him, was created in time from nothing. There was a time when the son was not, ran the theological slogan. It was the talk of the town in Alexandria, Greece, Asia Minor and Syria. No, shouted the orthodox. The son of God was uncreated and existed since all eternity. Their view prevailed at the first universal church Council in Nicaea in 325 CE, attended by the Emperor Constantine.

Subsequent major gatherings propelled themselves into even higher spheres of theological speculation. Did Christ consist of two separate persons, one divine, the other human, as the Syrian monk Nestorius suggested, or only in a single person, simultaneously wholly God and wholly man as defined by the Council of Ephesus in 431 CE? Twenty years later the Council of Chalcedon preferred to see two separate yet complete natures in the incarnate Jesus, thus repudiating the teaching of the Monophysites, dubbed heretical, that the limitless divine nature of Christ completely absorbed his finite humanity.

The best advice a non-Christian historian of Christianity can give is to go back to the authentic teaching of Jesus. Of course holders of all viewpoints would claim they are voicing just that.

Recently I have heard that the stance of the opponents of the ordination of women or homosexuals is based on the gospel of Jesus Christ. I would like to challenge them to quote the passages where Jesus outlawed the ordination of women, and he said nothing whatever about homosexuals. And if Jesus of Nazareth had sat incognito in the back row of the various councils, I doubt that he would have understood a word of the debates about his nature and person.

The authentic gospel of Jesus is still largely unperceived among church people: the message which the master from Nazareth – not Paul, John or two millennia of Christianity – formulated in his own language and teaching for his mostly uneducated Galilean Jewish audience.

172

27

The Evolution of Religious Ideas

Pope Benedict XVI's views on homosexuality and the use of condoms, echoed by the incoming head of the English Catholic church, Archbishop Nichols, invites reflection on the problem of the evolution of religious ideas among the heirs of Judaeo–Christian culture. For Jews the basic source of religious thinking is the Hebrew Bible and for Christians the Old and New Testaments. Scripture is read in both communities within their respective interpretative traditions. Yet despite the commonly professed subjection to scriptural guidance, one is puzzled by the diversity of understanding of the message of the Bible.

Take for instance progressive Catholic attitudes to the idea of creationism which is still vociferously propounded by fundamentalists of every denomination. In their view the biblical stories of the Book of Genesis are literally true. Is genuine Christianity obliged to adopt this position? 'No, it is not', we heard recently Cardinal Cormac Murphy O'Connor declare. Yet if he had given the same negative reply a century ago, he would have been obliged to face the growling Biblical Commission of the Vatican. Its decree of 30 June 1909, published in the official journal of the Roman church, forbad Catholics to question the historicity of the creation accounts in Genesis as they contained the 'objective reality and historical truth of events which really happened'. All one can conclude from the complete volte-face performed by a progressive Catholic is that the development of ideas during the last hundred years has been considerably faster than that of the species investigated by Darwin.

Such a conflict of ecclesiastical opinions immediately raises the question of the role of the Bible in the thinking of the peoples of 'the Book. Those who stick to a pre-Darwinian concept of the creation believe that the words of Scripture must be taken as Gospel truth wrapped in the infallible tradition of the religious authority. But grown-up believers long for probing questions rather than for a constant dishing out of ready-made answers. Indeed, those who permit science and reason to influence their world view dare utter the magic word, *reinterpretation*. A sensible move, think the moderates, but the summit of folly for Bible-bashers and slavish church devotees.

Another problem arises with the plurality of scriptural traditions, a common phenomenon already in the Hebrew Bible. For centuries after their conquest of the Holy Land around 1200 BCE the Jews offered sacrifices in temples located in the various cities of the land. But from the seventh century BCE onwards Jerusalem became the only legitimate place for worship, and engendered fresh legislation which remained valid even after the destruction of the Temple in 70 CE and prevented the Jews from building a new place of sacrificial worship anywhere else.

In the Gospels, too, we find two separate rulings about divorce. That given in Mark and Luke forbids divorce in all circumstances, but Matthew has an exception clause: divorce is permissible on the ground of the wife's unchastity. Even that moral rigorist, St Paul, allows a Christian spouse to remarry if the pagan partner refuses peacefully to cohabit with him or her. So it was up to Christian religious authorities to make their choice. Some outlaw divorce, others permit it in some cases.

A third eventuality arises when changed social circumstances cause contemporary ideas to clash with Scripture. The obvious examples are the ordination of women and homosexuality. Today's western society is inclined to sanction both. Yet the Bible provides no loopholes. There are no female apostles in the Gospels and St Paul positively silences women in the churches. (Traditionalism produces similar dictates in Judaism, too, making it inconceivable to have female rabbis in an orthodox synagogue.)

About homosexuality, while Jesus said nothing on the subject, no one could be more vituperative than Paul. Dare I quote him referring to 'degrading passions', to women exchanging natural intercourse for 'unnatural', and to men committing 'shameless acts with men'? Paul once managed to survive stoning by enraged Diaspora Jews; would he dare face the gay liberation front?

To solve the dilemma created by the clash between modern mentality and millennia old Holy Writ one must ask what Moses, Jesus or Paul would think, say or do if they lived today. Would Moses still speak of Israel as the only chosen people of God? Would Jesus announce the coming of the Kingdom and Paul the return of Christ during the lifetime of the current generation? What the present-day religious mind needs is pragmatic common sense.

This thought reminds me of an anecdote I read not long ago. Some years after the appearance of *On the Origin of Species*, Darwin's great nephew, the future composer Ralph Vaughan Williams, overheard the adults discussing the book. He asked his mother what all that argument was about. This was her significant reply: 'The Bible says that God made the world in six days. Great Uncle Charles thinks it took longer: but we need not worry about it, for it is *equally* wonderful either way.'

28

Let's Hope Vatican Politics Do Not Hinder the Holy Spirit

The conclave that is to elect the 265th successor of St Peter to the See of Rome will solemnly open today [17 April 2005]. The cardinals, so Catholics believe, will be guided by the Holy Spirit. However, the fact that 114 of the 117 qualified electors were appointed by John Paul II, most of them belonging to his conservative brand of Catholicism, does not facilitate the job of the Spirit. Nevertheless, it is to be hoped the divine *Paraclete* can exert an independent influence despite the odds he is faced with.

The late Pope casts a gigantic shadow on the conclave. His long pontificate was distinguished by a strenuous and successful effort that, with some mundane factors (the threat of the American star wars and the collapse of the Russian economy), led to the liberation of Eastern Europe from communism. John Paul was also a constant, though less successful, advocate of the case of the world's poor before the wealthy nations of the West. He furthermore distinguished himself by genuine openings towards other religions, including the Jews, to whom he expressed regret for centuries of Christian anti-Semitism. As a rule, his instincts were perfect, although their effect was sometimes quietly spoilt by crafty Vatican bureaucrats.

But there was also a darker side to the highly influential reign of John Paul II. As soon as the word conservative is mentioned, sex and gender problems spring into the limelight. In the wake of papal encyclicals, leading Catholic spokesmen have gone on trumpeting, though without much practical impact on a large segment of the faithful, the intrinsic immorality of artificial contraception. They have waged war on the use of condoms even as a defence against HIV. They have decried homosexuality as the worst abomination (though speaking sotto voce when the culprits were paedophile priests). Reform of divorce, the abolition of compulsory priestly celibacy and the ordination of women were adamantly rejected by John Paul II.

To judge both the legacy of John Paul II and the problems facing the new papacy, there should be one sure criterion – the teaching of Jesus. Is conservative Catholicism based on the gospel?

The answer of Church dignitaries would be unhesitatingly affirmative. But a look at the New Testament produces a picture that even they must find disturbing. Two thousand years ago, Jesus had no teaching about artificial birth control. Regarding the situation of the millions of AIDS victims, on past performance one can be sure Jesus would have shown to these latter-day 'lepers' his customary compassion and given them a helping hand.

Homosexuality no doubt existed in ancient Palestinian society, but it was not prominent and was never directly mentioned by Jesus. There is only one indirect reference to it in the Gospels, when Jesus declares the sinners of Sodom less guilty than the inhabitants of Capernaum, who paid no attention to his preaching. As for obligatory priestly celibacy, it certainly was not imposed by Jesus. His own apostles, including Peter, were not celibates. The priests of the Eastern Churches, even those in union with Rome, can marry, and even in the West priestly matrimony persisted until it was pronounced legally invalid by the Second Lateran Council in the twelfth century.

In his outlook of an impending arrival of God's reign, Jesus seems to have opposed divorce as an inappropriate move when so little time remained. But his message was already softened in the New Testament when Matthew made him announce that unchastity of a wife was a sufficient ground for dissolving a marriage. Again, there is not one word in the gospels to disqualify women from the priesthood. Indeed, Jesus never refers to Christian priests or bishops. Admittedly, his preaching companions were male, but this was the custom of his age.

We cannot ignore his many women friends, who turned out more reliable and courageous than his male apostles.

By the way, backing for substitute feminism, the cult of Mary, is next to none in the Gospels. Mark, Matthew and Luke almost entirely ignore Mary during the public life of Jesus, and the little they have to say is not positive. Jesus apparently had higher esteem for his disciples than for his family, including his mother. Only John, the latest of the evangelists, tries to rewrite the story by alluding to Mary at least at the wedding in Cana and at the cross.

Surprisingly, neither did Church matters occupy a central place in the thinking of Jesus. The word 'church' (*ekklesia*) is missing from Mark, Luke and John, and figures only in two, probably superadded, passages of Matthew.

It would be presumptuous for an outsider to offer advice to the conclave, but may he be allowed a dream? In this dream, the new Pope is urged by God to revitalize Catholicism from within by concentrating on the authentic gospel of Jesus, on the message conveyed by him to his disciples, and not on the doctrine about Jesus developed by St Paul and two millennia of Christianity. This is a simple and moving message, which Jesus formulated in his own language for his simple Galilean audience, about God, the heavenly Father, the dignity of all human beings as children of God, a life turned into worship by total trust, an overwhelming sense of urgency to do one's duty without delaying tactics, a sanctification of the here and now, and, yes, the love of God through the love of one's neighbour.

If made prominent, and not concealed under verbiage about sex, rituals, mass canonization of saints and Mary worship, the authentic gospel would concentrate on the true essence of religion, an existential relationship between human beings, and humanity and God.

Reconstructed with the tools of twenty-first-century historical and biblical scholarship, and perceived by twenty-first-century minds in twenty-first-century circumstances, it would appeal to thinking people all over the world, who have left the Church in droves, and feed a genuine ecumenical spirit among religious groups outside Catholicism.

There are cardinals in the conclave qualified to implement these ideas. Carlo Maria Martini, a liberal front runner, is one of the five learned editors of the most up-to-date scholarly version of the Greek New Testament, and Joseph Ratzinger used to be a progressive theologian before becoming John Paul's doctrinal enforcer at the head of the Vatican department formerly known as the Inquisition. Can the Holy Spirit persuade him to turn back to his original self? If not, there are many highly competent Catholic scripture interpreters and theologians who would gladly do the job should the chains placed on them during the past quarter of a century, like those of St Peter in Herod's prison, be miraculously removed.

29

Moving on from Reproach to Rapprochement

The Pope and the President of Israel

Next Thursday the son of the caretaker of a Jewish school in Tehran will pay a state visit to the son of a Bavarian policeman. In plain language, Moshe Katsav, President of Israel, will be received amid pomp and ceremony in the Vatican by Pope Benedict XVI.

Five years ago, during his pilgrimage to Jerusalem, Pope John Paul II placed a prayer on a piece of paper in a crack of the Western Wall, in which he expressed his sorrow for the ill-treatment of Jews by Christians. His moving gesture will be matched in poignancy when the hand of friendship is offered to a Jewish leader by the man who in his teens was obliged to join the Hitler Youth. The meeting will constitute, it is hoped, a fresh departure in the unhappy history of Catholic–Jewish relations.

The 1,900-year conflict between the two oldest monotheistic faiths belongs to the darkest and saddest chapters of the religious history of the Western world. The original catastrophe struck at 3pm on Friday, 7 April, 30 CE, when the charismatic Galilean religious preacher, Jesus of Nazareth, expired on a Roman cross, wrongly sentenced to death as an insurgent by the governor of Judaea, Pontius Pilate, with the connivance of the local Jewish leaders.

Within a few decades the followers of Jesus, by then largely non-Jews, recognized Jesus as Son of God and finally as God. As a result, for nearly two millennia the Church considered the Jews of all ages as guilty of the murder of God, the crime called deicide in Christian theology. From then on the Synagogue and the Church were engaged in a constant conflict filled with vituperation and

180

name-calling. Saintly Church Fathers had regular recourse to what would seem to us unparliamentary language. The 'gold-mouthed' St John Chrysostom, patriarch of Constantinople, described the Jewish synagogue in a sermon as 'a brothel, a brigands' cave and a wild beasts' den'.

To St Jerome, the only expert in Hebrew among fourth-century Christians, who gave us the Latin Vulgate translation of the whole Bible, worship in the synagogue sounded like 'the grunting of pigs and the braying of donkeys'.

Not unexpectedly the Jews responded in kind. In antiquity and in the Middle Ages they referred to Jesus as a magician and the bastard son of a Jewish hairdresser, Miriam, whom her husband divorced because of her adultery with a Roman soldier by the name of Panthera or Pandera. Many Jews blamed Jesus and the Christian Church for the bloody anti-Semitic outrages which occurred throughout the ages, from the pogroms organized by the medieval Crusaders in Germany to the Shoah, the Nazi Holocaust.

After the war the relationship between Christians and Jews began to improve. On the Jewish side, apart from substantial participation in the work of national and international councils of Christians and Jews, the main contribution came from scholars who set out to restore for Jewish perusal a denominationally unbiased picture of Jesus and Christianity.

Not many years ago, a well-known Israeli author, writing in the country's leading newspaper, called the age-old Jewish ban on the name of Jesus 'patently absurd'. In the Christian camp the courageous steps by the Roman Catholics deserve particular notice. In the Second Vatican Council (1962–5) – in which the young Joseph Ratzinger, the future Benedict XVI, busied himself as a progressive theological expert – cardinals and bishops decided, despite strong resistance from conservative quarters, formally to exculpate the Jews from the odium of being Christ-killers: 'Neither all the Jews at the time, nor the Jews today, can be charged with the crimes committed during the Passion.'

One of the most striking practical consequences of this purification of ideas appears in the revised Good Friday service of the Roman Catholics. The pre-Vatican II liturgy included supplications for various groups within the Church (the Pope, bishops, priests, the Emperor if there was one) as well as for heretics, schismatics and even pagans, but placed the Jews because of their *perfidia* (sinful faithlessness) in a distinct category. In their case the congregation was not invited to pray or bend the knee. The new liturgy removes the discrimination, and the celebrant entreats the Lord for the Jews, 'the first to hear the word of God, that they may continue to grow in the love of His name and in faithfulness to His covenant'.

Circumstances have surely changed but more improvement is needed on both sides. It is to be hoped that the Israeli President's visit to the Vatican at the initiative of the German Pope will mark a new move towards progress on a continuously deepening level. This progress will demand courage and strenuous effort.

Jews will have to stop being afraid of Jesus and treating him as taboo. When we look at him through the prism of history, rather than theology, and in the light of all the freshly gained knowledge of the world in which he lived, he reveals himself as Jesus the Jew, who in the judgment of Martin Buber, one of the greatest modern Jewish thinkers, deserves an 'important place in the religious history of Israel'.

The task Christians have to confront is, if anything, even more challenging. They must face up to the fact that the image of Jesus and the formulation of his message have come down to the Church not in their original language – they were delivered to simple Aramaic-speaking Galilean Jews – but in a culturally alien language (Greek) and in a form adapted to the needs of Hellenized non-Jews of Syria, Egypt, Asia Minor, Greece and Rome. The saying *Tradutore traditore* (a translator is a traitor) applies not just to texts but to the transmission of religious ideas as well. Christians need to discover the Jewish meaning of the authentic message preached and practised by Jesus and a way to apply them to their own circumstances today. Take his command to behave like children of God. Jesus does not advocate childishness, a lack of self-confidence and a constant demand for help and mediation from priests, saints, the Virgin Mary or even from himself – but recommends his own Jewish notion of a son of God, which entails boundless trust in the heavenly Father who can be reached directly by all his children. Such an outlook may turn out to be more exciting than the humdrum doctrine which churchgoers quite often hear from the pulpit.

During the past three decades, scholars on both the Jewish and the Christian sides have made great advances in clearing the path for a new understanding of Jesus and his gospel. Will Christian leaders and teachers of today and tomorrow be lion-hearted enough to come to grips with the challenge that beckons?

Acknowledgment of Sources

For permission to republish previously published items, I would like to thank the following:

'The Age of Jesus', first published in Geza Vermes, 2005, *Who's Who in the Age of Jesus*, London: Penguin.

'Jesus the Jew', lecture at the *Ways with Words* Literature Festival, Dartington Hall, Devon, 8 July 2001.

'The Changing Faces of Jesus in the New Testament and Since', lecture to the Hungarian Academy of Science, 8 June 2001, on the occasion of the launch of the Hungarian edition of *The Changing Faces of Jesus*.

'Jesus God in Spite of Himself', first published in French by *Le Point* on 22 September 2005.

'When You Strip Away All the Pious Fiction, What is Left of the Real Jesus?', first published in *The Times*, 24 December 2004.

'Jesus Was a Great Man', first published in the *Independent*, 8 April 2001.

'Benedict XVI and Jesus of Nazareth: A Review', first published in *The Times*, 19 May 2007.

'The Truth about the Historical Jesus', first published in *Standpoint*, September 2008.

'A Television Documentary on Christ and the British Press: Channel 4's *Jesus: the Evidence* (April 1984)', first published in *Lycidas* (Wolfson College, Oxford) in 1986.

'The Nativity Narratives Seen by a Historian', first published in *History Today*, December 2006.

'Matthew's Nativity is Charming and Frightening . . . But It's a Jewish Myth', first published in the *Sunday Telegraph*, 18 December 2004.

'Celluloid Brutality', first published in the *Guardian*, 7 February 2004.

'The Passion', lecture at the Hay on Wye Literary Festival, 2005.

'Caiaphas Was Innocent?', first published in the *Sunday Telegraph*, 15 February 2004.

'Iscariot and the Dark Path to the Field of Blood', first published in *The Times*, 8 April 2006.

'The Resurrection', first published in *The Times*, 6 April 2009.

'Secrets of the Scrolls', first published in *The Times*, 27 December 1991.

'Exploring the Scross', first published as 'Dead Sea Scrolls' in *Standpoint*, May 2009.

'The Qumran Community and the Essenes', lecture delivered in Oxford, 2 June 2009.

'Midrash in the Dead Sea Scrolls and the New Testament', lecture at BAJS, Yarnton Manor, 12 July 2004.

'The Notion of the Covenant in the Dead Sea Scrolls', lecture, Yarnton Manor, 18 October 2006.

'Tax-Collectors', first published in Polish in *Tygodnik Prowszechny*, 6 March 2006.

'Christian Origins in a Nutshell', first published in French in *Le Point* (Hors série 11–12), 2006.

'The Great *Da Vinci Code* Distraction', first published in *The Times*, 6 May 2004.

'What's Sex Got to Do with It?', first published in the *Guardian*, 29 November 2003.

'The Evolution of Religious Ideas', first published in the *Guardian* online, 22 April 2009.

'Let's Hope Vatican Politics Do Not Hinder the Holy Spirit', first published in the *Daily Telegraph*, 17 April 2005.

'Moving on from Reproach to Rapprochement: the Pope and the President of Israel', first published in *The Times*, 12 November 2005.